Dedication
To Ivan Bezugloff,
for his ecouragement and like-mindedness.
Gratefully,
Susan Medenica 2015

Xenophon Press Library

Xenophon Press is dedicated to the preservation
of classical equestrian literature.

30 Years with Master Nuno Oliveira, Michel Henriquet 2011
A New Way to Dress Horses, Cavendish 2016
A Rider's Survival from Tyranny, Charles de Kunffy 2012
Another Horsemanship, Jean-Claude Racinet, 1994
Art of the Lusitano, Yglesias de Oliveira, 2012
Austrian Art of Riding, Werner Poscharnigg 2015
Baucher and His School, General Decarpentry 2011
Dressage in the French Tradition, Dom Diogo de Bragança 2011
École de Cavalerie Part II, Expanded Ed. de la Guérinière 2015
Equine Osteopathy: What the Horses Have Told Me, Giniaux 2014
François Baucher: The Man and His Method, Baucher/Nelson, 2013
Great Horsewomen of the 19th Century in the Circus, Nelson 2014
Gymnastic Exercises for Horses Volume II, Eleanor Russell 2013
H. Dv. 12 Cavalry Manual of Horsemanship, Reinhold 2014
Healing Hands, Dominique Giniaux, DVM 1998
Horse Training: Outdoors and High School, Beudant 2014
Legacy of Master Nuno Oliveira, Stephanie Millham 2013
Methodical Dressage of the Riding Horse, Faverot de Kerbrech 2010
Racinet Explains Baucher, Jean-Claude Racinet 1997
The Art of Riding a Horse, d'Eisenberg 2015
The Art of Traditional Dressage, Volume I DVD, de Kunffy 2013
The Dressage Way, Medenica 2015
The Ethics and Passions of Dressage Expanded Ed., de Kunffy 2013
The Gymnasium of the Horse, Gustav Steinbrecht 2011
The Italian Tradition of Equestrian Art, Tomassini 2014
The Maneige Royal, Antoine de Pluvinel 2010, 2015
The Portuguese School of Equestrian Art, de Oliveira/da Costa, 2012
The Science and Art of Riding in Lightness, Stodulka 2014
The Spanish Riding School & Piaffe and Passage, Decarpentry 2013
Total Horsemanship, Jean-Claude Racinet 1999
Truth in the Teaching of Master Nuno Oliveira, Eleanor Russell 2015
Wisdom of Master Nuno Oliveira, Antoine de Coux 2012

Available at www.XenophonPress.com

The Dressage Way

by SUSAN MEDENICA

© Xenophon Press 2015

XENOPHON PRESS

The Dressage Way

by Susan Medenica

Copyright © 2015 by Xenophon Press LLC

Edited by Richard F. Williams

All rights reserved. No part of this work may be reproduced or transmitted in any form or by any means, electronic or mechanical, including photocopying, or by any information storage or retrieval system except by a written permission from the publisher.

Published by Xenophon Press LLC

7518 Bayside Road, Franktown, Virginia 23354-2106, U.S.A.

XenophonPress@gmail.com

ISBN-13: 9780933316782

Cover image by Artist, Liz Wiley, Copyright © 2014 www.LizWiley.com

Introduction

How much is in a word? How much can you ask of it and where does it lead?

Within this book of three parts, I have chosen to change only one two-letter word in each title. It is a big job these little words have been given: nothing less than to portray the evolution of the trainer as she makes her journey from beginning to end.

In the first section, the preposition "of" denotes the forthright attitude of beginning. It is the trainer finding and entering upon the path. It is the trainer at a sometimes naive distance from her subject, initiating the relationship.

The title of the second section contains the word "to." This is a statement of direction, a more personal view of the journey. It is the trainer within the process, using her means to confront the uncertainty of becoming. It is the trainer testing her knowledge within the now familiar reality of the horse.

And finally, within the title of the third section, there appears the word "is." What power. What audacity. What simplicity. The discovery has been made: that the trainer's path is dressage and conversely, that dressage is the path. This is a bold equation, almost religious, in which the trainer has at last included herself in the larger world. There is now no "against," only "with." At one and the same time she has become both larger and smaller: larger by virtue of knowledge, smaller because of still greater knowledge; of herself, of the horse. It is her mature intimacy with nature in which she finds and defines herself.

Within these three sets of essays, I have attempted to relate what it is like to become a trainer. First, there is dressage without you. Then, there is you entering dressage. And finally, there is dressage with you. And to you it should be said: always the thinking mind, the refining mind, the testing mind, the concluding mind. That is the way.

— Susan Medenica

The Way of Dressage

Table of Contents

	Preface	9
Chapter 1	The Laws of Nature	10
Chapter 2	What is "Classical" Dressage?	18
Chapter 3	What is Classical Dressage?	25
Chapter 4	Meditation for the Dressage Rider	27
Chapter 5	Geometry of the Arena	32
Chapter 6	Go Forward, Be Round	34
Chapter 7	The Half-Halt	36
Chapter 8	One-Handed Riding	39
Chapter 9	Riding *Sans* Stirrups	41
Chapter 10	A Good Conversation	44
Chapter 11	Movement	47
Chapter 12	Observations from Work in-Hand	49
Chapter 13	Shape-Shifting	53
Chapter 14	Letting Go	58
Chapter 15	Making the Connection	62

Preface

The following collection of essays embodies an attempt to put into words the honest experience of dressage. It is not meant to be a technical treatise, which would be too limiting, nor an abstract philosophy, which would be unfounded, but an expression of unshakable faith in dressage as the art of balance between two dissimilar creatures, between thought and action, between head and heart. The practice should be nothing less.

Written essentially from two different points of view, each piece is either the voice of the instructor or that of the trainer. That they are two sides of the same impulse should not be forgotten since it is endemic to the process of dressage that to instruct the rider is to influence and consequently train the horse. The subjects treated, therefore, range from the well defined "What is Classical Dressage?" to the more ephemeral "Shape-Shifting" and as such, encompass the infinite breadth of what dressage can aspire to. In this spirit, it is the hope that the thoughts expressed will inspire each reader to undertake a more personal and profound journey with his most noble guide, the horse.

The Laws of Nature

When Classicists talk of a return to the "laws of nature," they are referring to certain principles assumed to be worthy of attention if not downright adoration. Balance, symmetry, harmony, and proportion are all linked to these "laws," but in fact, are more man's idealized version of nature than nature itself.

The Western view of nature presents itself as a complex combination of appreciation for its raw beauty and antagonism toward its independence. We are both in awe of what we can't control yet passionate in our desire to control it. In some way we recognize we are a part of this natural world but at the same time, strive to place ourselves above it. We possess the "power of reason," after all. No wonder we were placed here to have dominion over not only the beasts of the field but the field as well.

By virtue of the Western reliance on the "power of reason," we have distanced ourselves from the natural world. All aberrant, non-man-like reason is diminished in value and relegated to man's recreation not of actual reality, but of his failed attempt at reality. The elevation of man's "reason" over all other and particular perceptions of existence is, of course, self-delusion. Reason per se does not exist apart from man's invention of it.

The Eastern view of nature, however, is not so much a view as it is a way to be. "Being" is not removed to a comfortable distance from nature where it can be surgically examined, qualified, and mastered. Instead, man's being is integrated into nature, flowing with but never apart from its stream of reality. Being, quite simply, allows for breath; it allows for quick change. It allows for individual identity; it allows for universal identity. In short, the "being" view of the East endures precisely because it does not diminish in value the animate urge and instead, celebrates and goes along with its vast display within the workings of nature.

In the East, nature is not separate from man nor does man place himself outside of nature. Man is a part of nature as nature is a part of man. The two are one. Imbalance occurs when man does not recognize this obligatory law.

So what does this have to do with the classical training of the dressage horse? In a word, everything. The teachings of the old masters were and continue to be based on the horse as a natural creature complete with his own obedience to certain "natural" laws. "Whatever is forced cannot be beautiful," states Xenophon, 400 B.C., and indeed the classical principles arise from man's longing to enter into the natural world through the horse. It is as if the disparity between them vanishes through the mutual respect each accords the other in this enlightened collaboration. But first, an examination of scrupulous honesty must take place. It is the duty of the trainer to have no illusions about who the horse is. This is not the place for wishful thinking. This is, however, the place for the trainer to undergo profound change as he strives for truth. After all, the horse is quite perfect at being a horse. We, however, face continual struggle to become the trainer the horse needs us to be. The truth resides in our ability to learn from the horse, our ability to change, and most important, our undeviating desire to be with the horse with as little disturbance to his unique expression as possible. This is how he touches us.

The first law of nature is that the horse is neither good nor bad; he is quite simply, a horse. He has his particular view of existence and behaves according to his own "animate urge." Furthermore, he is always exemplary at being a horse, taking pleasure in what he does best and personally celebrating his own abilities. And ultimately, the horse is able to accomplish this quite apart from us. He needs no validation. Startling as this may be to accept, it is the gateway to honest collaboration with the horse and is a prerequisite for growth.

For the trainer, this poses a knotty problem, often one that cannot be easily overcome with conventional western thinking. If the horse is indeed neither good nor bad, then who is at fault when something goes awry? "Aha! There is no one else here, so it must be me. But that's not possible. He's only a horse after all, I am the trainer."

How many times we put the onus on the horse. It is the automatic, reflexive way out of absolute honesty. If the horse is not to blame, then I must take on the blame myself and that would lower my status as a trainer, not in the eyes of the horse necessarily, but certainly in the eyes of other trainers. My needy baby bird ego would suffer so I will shift the blame to the horse and thereby rise in importance.

This is, in essence, the stumbling block: to perceive the horse as neither good nor bad. It challenges the hierarchal view of man and animal and breaks down long held beliefs and cherished ideals of the superiority of man and his machinations, his god-given right to rule over the "beasts of the field" and indeed, over any of his own that he considers beasts. But whatever we believe, whatever we falsify for our own gain, however we feel ourselves, the horse remains neither good nor bad but perfect – at being a horse.

Who then is this model of perfection, our guide in understanding natural laws? Law #2 states that the horse is a prey animal. He is subject to instant panic and prefers to flee if he can, rather than confront. His cellular knowledge tells him that at the least suspicion, he should be off and running. This is how he lives another day. This is how he stays around and secures his continued existence.

For our purposes as trainers, this is essential knowledge. To understand the excitability of the horse, his susceptibility to outside influence is at the core of dealing with him. If he is so responsive to his environment, it follows that as part of his environment, he should also be responsive to me and here is the dilemma faced by many a trainer: convincing the horse that we are a part of his environment, yet not that part which he should flee from. We need his attention, not his distraction. We need his interest and curiosity, not his fear.

Ingratiating ourselves to the horse leads us directly to law #3: the horse is a herd animal. He operates in a rather tightly knit social group, one which allows for the ebb and flow of interaction without harm or destruction to its members. It is a model society, allowing not only for continued well being of the group, but also giving rise to friendships of varying intensities within that group. The herd is a comfortable place for a horse, a place he would rather be than not. He will always try to return to it in time of stress.

For the trainer, dealing with the horse's attachment to a herd is the fundamental problem to be faced. Whether it is the weaning of a youngster or separation of an older horse from a favorite buddy, being alone is an emotional ordeal for the horse. But alas, it is an ordeal the horse must pass through not only for our convenience in dealing with him, but more importantly, it is our prime opportunity for teaching the horse transference: how to substitute his reliance on the herd to a reliance on us.

Reliance implies subordination and points directly to law #4: the horse seeks a leader. Horses are hierarchal, but loosely so and adapt, though not without some upheaval, to changing circumstance: introduction or removal of a horse from the group, maturation of an individual, gestation and birth, an outside enemy, weather and climate, and availability of food and water. As such, decisions are constantly being made and the leader tested as to the wisdom of those decisions. What the leader dictates is what the others obey. When the others do not obey, the leader is no longer the designated leader and another emerges as need demands.

This is significant knowledge for a trainer to heed and is not as simple as it at first appears. Though the individual horse will seek to be a leader himself and will test your capabilities in that regard, he is quite content to be in a lower position in the hierarchy as long as he knows who is above him and who is below him. So the common notion of dominating the horse is at least partially correct. The horse who accepts a leader, whether that leader is equine or human, is not confused. He knows where he belongs. Profound difficulties arise, however, when the leader does not recognize his responsibility toward the horse for making him secure. Certainly the horse leader imparts this sense of security to the band and demonstrates the quality of benevolent leadership by conferring the benefits of safety and non-threatened ease of existence on the members. Can the human trainer say the same of his leadership? If domination is the sole quality of the trainer's leadership the horse will not trust. If the horse does not trust, he will not be comfortable. If he is not comfortable, he will not learn. And so it goes that the prime responsibility of the trainer is to never act unjustly toward his charge and to make it his constant obsession to become ever more just in his dealings through self-effacing refinement of his own self. The trainer must master himself first before he can master the horse.

And just why is this so? Law #5 has it that the horse is an anxious creature, demonstrating an underlying shyness and reticence toward his environment. Far from the mighty, bigger-than-life steed of our imaginations, the horse is at the core, timid and easily upset. How he has become dulled and disinterested through his dealings with humans does not belie the fact that the horse by himself and from the very first, reacts immediately, then, at a safe distance, mulls it over and weighs the accuracy of his reaction.

The task of the trainer is to make the horse comfortable within himself because he understands that the trainer is both his master and his servant. The ongoing problem for the trainer is when to be which. Too much one way or the other, or even worse, being fluent in only one of these qualities will produce anxiety which in turn will lead to unwanted behaviors in the horse. The best way to avoid this situation is to not seek it in the first place and at all attempts to comfort the horse by being exact in your perceptions of his emotional state and your actions in dealing with it. Anxiety in the horse is produced by him not knowing where he belongs. The more you can calm and reassure him that his position with you is stable and that he is safe as "second in command," the more eagerly he will take the training and display the curiosity and demeanor so basic to the relaxed horse. Relaxed equals receptive in the horse.

For the trainer, it is essential to comprehend the workings of the horse before undertaking his education and toward this, one of the most important laws is #6: the horse is a master of time and space. By this we understand that he does not differentiate between the two but perceives time and space as part of the same experience so that "his time has substance, his pace has duration." This fusion of dimensions is connected in turn to three dominant behaviors of the horse: his absolute adherence to a life of energy efficiency, his resistance to restriction, and his inclination toward routine or habit through conditioning.

To the horse then, communication from the trainer must adhere to the no history/no future perception of the horse. Like it or not, the horse lives in the moment, the moment, the moment, each following each in an ever-changing realization of movement. Again, the horse exists in time (the moment), in space (the movement), with no difference between the two.

If this seems like heady stuff, it is, because while we are standing back and analyzing the horse, he is well on his way to the next moment and the next and the next and so on, leaving our busy little minds spinning in the past. Typically, we then jump ahead of him into the future and again, we are not with him, but waiting anxiously, biding our time while he catches up and instantly moves beyond us. Too early, too late, too early too late; it is constant frustration for the human who sincerely desires to be with the horse not to mention for the horse to whom this leapfrogging is frustrating as well. In order to be with the horse then, where and when we deliver our messages becomes the difference between failure of the horse to understand and his compliance with our wishes. Where and when to him are the same. We are in essence directing moment by moment through space, within time as these dimensions meet within the horse. As such, we find ourselves in no time, occupying fleeting space, both evaporating as if they never were and never will be. We are then with the horse.

Where the horse is at any given moment in space suggests to the trainer how and when to use the aids and further reveals that the aids given to the horse comprise a sort of circulatory system. What the leg does (go) reflects forward to the hand. What the hand does (stop) reflects to the leg, and in the middle is the horse. Viewed in this manner, the aids allow for an infinite number of ways to talk to the horse with inspiration and precision. The vocabulary expands precisely because it has the non-differentiated space and time in which to do so; the original flow of all living things undisturbed.

From the esoteric, we move into the more physical plane of law #7: the alert horse will raise his head and neck, thereby hollowing his back. Like the pulling back of a bowstring, alertness tightens the horse in preparation for instant reaction. In terms of dressage, it also disengages the horse with the haunches behind the body mass so that the horse is in three different places at once: the head and neck above, the conduit of the back below, and the haunches behind. While this may work for the horse out on the open plains, this "up, periscope" position is far from efficient for the ridden horse.

As trainers, we deal with the horse's natural alertness all the time. In fact, it is a continual contest to win his attention away from his infinitely interesting surroundings and bring it back on us. How well we do this determines our success as trainers and all too often our failures as students of the horse. Stimulus then, whether from the environment or from us, will cause the horse to string himself tight and focus intently on that stimulus.

To further explain, whenever the trainer asks for an "up" transition, a change of direction, a transition from straight to sideways, more impulsion, in short, any change, the horse's immediate response will be to raise his head and neck in alertness. This is, after all, in part what we want. He has received the message. The next message we give him is crucial and leads directly to the companion law, law #8: the relaxed horse lowers his head and neck thereby stretching his topline and raising his back.

We are fortunate that the "down and round" position of the horse's head and neck is both a subordinate and a relaxing position for the horse. The horse assumes this position on his own accord when he grazes and dozes, and by our request when we ask for his attention. It is the position of relaxed focus for the horse and the position we return the horse to over and over again, reminding him that the world can be a comfortable place, even when the human makes seemingly unreasonable demands.

Together, the alert horse and relaxed horse positions make up the horse we ride and together, they deliver the "go forward, be round" message. By cleverly availing ourselves of these two energy intensities, and their exponential possibilities, we can pretty much shape the horse in whatever way we wish. Between the leg which excites and the hand which calms are thus the boundaries within which the horse performs and within which the only limitation is the trainer's creativity.

As a prey animal, it is the alert horse who gets away but it is previous and cumulative relaxation that fuels the flight. Law #9 states that: the horse is a model of energy conservation and will make decisions accordingly. The life of a grazing animal is by and large a life of meandering from one plentiful patch of grass to the next, spending most waking time in this deliberate endeavor. Slow, stretched, languid movement characterizes the grazing horse who appears almost aimless in his course. This, of course, is not the case for it is by design that the horse is not only fueled by grazing but also accumulates energy and to a certain extent, supplies his body for quick movement when needed.

For the trainer, meeting the deeply ingrained food-getting behavior in the horse without knowing where it comes from can often lead to exclamations of the "Why is he so slow, dumb, unresponsive?" These are by no means totally unjustified feelings but have little to do with the task at hand which is to get a desired response from the horse.

When mounted for the first time, unless fear is present, most if not all horses will stand still, crane their heads and necks around to sniff a toe or to look at this distantly familiar creature now on their backs. Most will not move forward and this is the essence of the horse: unless he is compelled by fear or threat of punishment, he will avoid all expenditures of energy that do not relate directly to his survival. He is not lazy; he is, in fact, obeying a higher directive within himself. This is not to imply that the trainer needs to make the horse fearful of him to get forward movement. Far from it. The horse will move when he understands that is what is wanted of him and that he can do it without losing his sense of balance and comfort.

Nothing in nature is symmetrical and the horse is no exception. Law #10 states that: the horse is not absolutely symmetrical right to left as reflected in both his structure and his range of motion. For the horse, his sidedness is a non-issue since he is a creature of the open plains where turns, circles, and straight lines do not exist. He is, however, balanced for the job he has to do apart from man: negotiate varied terrain, sprint away at any inkling of danger, and infallibly choose the line of least resistance in his reactions.

When we put the horse and man together, however, things of necessity have to change not only for the benefit of the horse, but also to satisfy man's well-intentioned attempts to manipulate what he finds objectionable in nature. What happens all too often is that the trainer artificially adjusts the horse so that he fits the stereotype of symmetry: equality of form and movement on both sides of an imaginary plumb line. This can clearly never be possible unless man intrudes to the point of warping out of recognition, what is natural for the horse. His strength and amplitude of gaits will always be different, his bend and tempo will always vary depending on what hand he is traveling. Even in the straight, "square" halt, the horse will carry slightly more on one side than the other. What is possible, however, is to enhance what is natural for each horse with the differences in sides giving rise to new ways of looking at, appreciating, and improving expressive movement. Absolute symmetry is not "natural;" we always ride two different horses at a time.

All living creatures without exception display an "animate urge" as they fulfill their lives. What this implies is that each creature has a sense of his own identity, his own particular self, and the path he must follow, the space he must occupy. Law #11 states: when a hand or leg exerts pressure, the horse will respond by pushing against that pressure. In other words, he must be taught to give.

To the horse, the implication of this law is profound and manifests nothing less than his very existence, his assertion of self. When the space he occupies is invaded, the horse will push out the offender. This is no less so when the offender is the hand or leg of the trainer.

So as trainers, the first means of entry to the horse's world is through the morally questionable idea of the horse's loss of liberty, his surrender to us in order for us both to contribute to a mutually understandable language. Obviously, this is a decision not made by the horse. Be that as it may, when viewed from the language perspective, the loss of liberty seems not so much a loss as an open possibility for more self-expression from the horse. We can only trust that this is so.

Teaching the horse to give or to cede his space is the beginning of our control over the horse. The reason for its likely success is that between horses, the horse who moves the other horse in the herd is the leader. In other words, we become the bigger horse by getting our horse to move his shoulders, haunches, neck, and head. By giving, he in turn not only understands but acknowledges our role as leader and acquiesces his space accordingly.

In the horse's world, there is not only the space around him, but the space within his body that he is supremely aware of. Manipulation of either of these spaces, from outside by a fence or stall, or directly on the horse by use of the aids leads to the final law, law #12 which states: when restrained by the hand and leg together, the horse will contract. In other words, too much rigidity or containment will prevent the horse from going forward and will break the continuity of his topline so that he will not be round. When he is not round, the aids will not go through. When the aids do not go through, the horse is not in a place where he is likely to be trained.

Understand then, that each aid is like a door. If the door is open, the horse will go through it. If the door is closed, the horse will not progress past it. If all the doors are closed at once, the horse will contract. If all the doors are open at once, the horse will come apart. It is by the skillful use of opening and closing that the horse both goes forward and assumes roundness.

Contraction within the horse is thus produced by the simultaneous use of the aids wherein the legs and hands do isometrics against each other with the horse in the middle. Contraction is neither forward nor round but hesitant and angular. When no door is open for even an instant, the horse inside the aids does not resonate with vigor and intent.

Conclusion

An examination of the "laws of nature" is nothing more than an objective observation of what the horse as representative of nature is without the intrusion of man: how does he behave individually, what is his social structure, what code does he follow as the foundation of his existence?

From the resonance of the objective we can't help but be moved into the subjective realm when we recognize those same qualities within us though often too deeply subjugated to be able to come to the surface. What classical dressage does for us then, is meld the natural horse with the artificial man to produce something quite distinct: a union where each is balanced into existence by the other. In reality, each comes into self-carriage by virtue of the other and along a path which must of necessity include an acknowledgement of the "laws of nature." And this is how we enter into wholeness.

WHAT IS "CLASSICAL" DRESSAGE?

Introduction to the Word

How much can we expect of a word? Does the use of it show an increase in our understanding? Or do we bandy it about when we can think of no other word to satisfy a situation? Particularly when a word carries weight, its fate is often to become popularized to the point of dilution. Such a word is the word "Classical."

What does "Classic Coke" have to do with "Classical" dressage? Not much except in the most basic definition: "the best of its kind." This is the way it is used to describe certain dressage riders or horses when we wish to highlight them above the rest. "Best" is not good enough. "Classic" is better and seems to set the rider/horse/soda apart from their peers in a distinguished way.

Webster defines "Classical" in this way:

1. Of the highest rank or class
2. Having lasting significance or recognized worth
3. An outstanding representative of its kind; model
4. A work of the highest rank or excellence

Certainly advertisers would argue that Coke measures up to each of these definitions. If they didn't, the potential consumer would be justifiably suspect. "If it's the best of its kind, then obviously I must be a part of it. I'll have a Classic Coke please." And the product is marketed.

So how much can we expect of a word when the word in question is "Classical?" Plenty, if taken out of the simplistic albeit convenient environment of Webster.

History of the Word

Originally, the term "Classical" in western thought referred to a return to "the ideals of nature" as exemplified by the architecture, sculpture, drama, poetry, and music of ancient Greece and Rome. In short, "Classical" had to do with the best of its kind for all time. As seen by later generations, these ideals were something to recapture and bring into the Renaissance and Classical periods of art in western Europe. "Classical" dressage begins in ancient Greece (circa. 400 B.C.) with the principles set forth by Xenophon in his work, *The Art of Horsemanship*. It is given rebirth in the Renaissance and Classical periods (circa. 15th-19th centuries) in the works of Pluvinel, de la Guérinière, the Duke of Newcastle, Decarpentry, and later, in the more modern masters such as Steinbrecht, Fillis, Baucher, and Museler.

When formulating a definition of the word "Classical," and especially as it pertains to the riding and training of the dressage horse, Webster leaves much to be desired. Instead, the areas of philosophy and aesthetics, (the study of beauty), provide a way of exploring and determining just exactly what is and what is not "Classical." These are some rather rigorous criteria to uphold when fulfilling the definition, but without such intense attention, the word and its potential become hollow and superficial; in short, powerless to convey its original meaning.

Definition of "Classical"

So what then did the ancient Greeks have in mind when they invented the word? In typical academic fashion, they came up with seven concepts which had to be met before a work would be considered to be "Classical." Inasmuch as these seven concepts pertain to any work of art, they are not specifically aimed at the horse and rider but they offer the foundation from which we can narrow our focus more precisely to the horse and his training. Representative of the "ideals of nature," these seven concepts are a way of expressing that which nature has to teach us; nothing less.

1. The first quality of the "Classical" is **durability**. The Classic work is ageless and maintains its value through time. It is not diminished by temporal considerations and is itself a kind of everlasting testament to that nature which surrounds us entirely and for always.

2. Second, the quality of **profundity** must be inherent in the work. The "Classical" offers levels of meaning which may not always be immediately apparent and are not supposed to be. The outer is only a reflection of the inner. As it pertains to dressage, the horse is already representative of the "natural world" and as such, possesses below the surface and within himself, a kind of microcosm of that which exists in all of nature. Profound indeed.

3. As might be expected, **universality** is at the core of what is "Classical." The "Classical" speaks to all regardless of time or place. The language spoken evokes an underlying commonality among all people for all time and harkens back to the belief that the representation of the natural world will find resonance in each person.

4. The ancient Greek culture saw in the natural world, the embodiment of beauty and as such, believed that the "Classical" must demonstrate

aesthetic intent. Without beauty, there could be no honest and fulfilling connection to nature. The form versus function debate would have been a strange notion to the ancient Greeks since form to them was not a matter of practical utility but a quest for beauty revealed.

5. Whether the work in question is a sculpture, poem, or the training of the dressage horse, **technical prowess** should be evident in all aspects of the creation. The mastery of the medium, it should go without saying, is an indication of the successful deliverance of the message. Technique is a prerequisite and understood. Its fate, however, is to fade into the background and let the message of the work emerge. Artfulness or technique for its own sake is not enough. It must serve the master: thought, idea, message.

6. The "Classical" work is one of **completeness**. In and of itself it needs no explanation or assistance. It is a totality, an entity unto itself and a perfect model of the "natural world" as received through the eyes of mortals. It is a synthesis of what is and what is seen, thus uniting man with the "natural world."

7. And finally, the "Classical" work must contain **evidence of vision.** It must rise above the ordinary, the everyday, and deal with the eternal truths of the "natural world." The bridge between the prosaic and the everlasting was thus a kind of affirmation of the world apart from the human but only through vision could it be apprehended. Man's vision was the vehicle by which the abundant natural beauty was witnessed and transformed into the works of art from antiquity.

From these seven qualities inherent in the "Classical," we can see that the ancient Greeks appreciated both embodiment and the spirit that coexisted in the "natural world" and that the representation of that duality was of the more noble aspirations. They were well aware that the work of art was an amalgam of these two qualities and so it was that they approached their relationship with the horse.

Introduction to Classical Dressage

At the foundation of the training of the horse was of course his usefulness as a means of conveyance. He was the animal men trusted their lives to in battle and as such, had to be not only submissive to the will of the rider but compassionate enough to serve even when the rider gave him little assistance. From this, we can see that something more was exemplified by the horse than mere usefulness: his sovereignty. The Greeks held a deep appreciation for the nature of the horse and in their work with the horse, sought to be with him but not so much so as to rob him of his natural beauty. The ideal was therefore, one of partnership: a mutually satisfying government between two unlike creatures for the betterment of both.

History of Classical Dressage

As the qualities of the "Classical" pertain to horsemanship, they were much admired and followed by subsequent generations of trainers through the Renaissance and beyond. The schism that we now witness between "Classical" and competitive dressage comes not in any evolutionary sense but in the minds of men. What was once a necessity, (the thorough training of the horse for battle), became the training of the horse for the sheer beauty of the act. From the equestrian displays of the ancient Greeks to the fetes and carousels of the Renaissance and Classical periods in the royal courts of Europe, the horse was a means of artistic expression. In the nineteenth and early twentieth centuries, the court sponsored galas were replaced by circuses which always featured at least one performance of "haute école" riding in addition to liberty acts and acrobatics on the horse. No less luminaries than Fillis and Baucher appeared regularly in the circus and demonstrated the aesthetic of the horse through piaffe, passage, tempi changes, pirouettes, three-legged canters, Spanish walks and trots, and various samplings of the "airs above the ground." This was in no way "small" dressage and until the beginning of the twentieth century and the advent of competitive dressage sponsored by the military, was virtually the only place to witness the legacy of the ancient Greek notion of "beauty for beauty's sake."

When competition entered the picture, however, beauty was overshadowed by accuracy and so the competition horse was judged not so much on whether he displayed the ideal but whether he did a particular movement in a designated spot. This was, after all, a far easier way to measure the training than dealing with the sometimes imprecise and misunderstood areas of the ideal.

What has come about in dressage, therefore, is a deadlock between those who view it as a sport and those ever-increasing numbers who view it as an art. The artistic camp maintains competition places the horse in an unnatural frame, questions the "gimmicky" training methods, and generally under-appreciates the more scientific way of evaluating a horse's performance. The competitive camp, on the other hand, values the game well done, and questions the validity of a performance that cannot be measured objectively. Such it seems that the two will never come to an agreement since both the means and the goals are at odds.

The Ideals of Classical Dressage

Be that as it may, when assessing the riding and training of the dressage horse as "Classical" or not, there are ideals by which to judge. These ideals are engendered by the "natural world" vision of antiquity and espoused by subsequent trainers and riders who wished to find their place within this grand plan. (Some of these ideals will necessarily overlap into and refer back to the qualities of the "Classical" but are focused particularly on the horse and his training.)

1. The first ideal to be met is **balance**. Whether on four feet, two feet, or between the horse and rider, balance provides the stability necessary for movement. Without it, nothing more than the most rudimentary of actions can be achieved. Balance is not static, but ever-changing through space as the movement dictates. It is the flux of breath.

2. Second is the ideal of **harmony**, again, both within the horse and within the rider, and then, between the two. The union of horse and rider creates an entirely new entity with a new need to locate that point of amity between them. That point of amity is harmony.

3. Next comes the ideal of **grace**. "Whatever is forced cannot be beautiful" and it is the charm or beauty of the movement which elicits grace. The further definition of grace moves it into the realm of religion as being blessed or favored. Certainly a horse and rider moving in a state of grace is something more than mere charm and through the connection they have between each other, appear to be favored by the gods.

4. When we speak of **symmetry**, we are referring to a form being similar on either side of a dividing line. In the case of the horse when viewed from the side, is he ridden in three equal pieces? As is most often the case, the horse is too short in the neck with the haunches trailing out behind by virtue of a misunderstood collection. When viewed from the top, or from side to side, it is the rare horse who even through advanced training, exhibits either proportionate stance or movement from one side to the other. But it is the goal of "Classical" dressage to create a horse equal on both sides, symmetrical back to front.

5. **Rhythm** is possibly one of the more important measures of the ideal for it is through rhythm that the horse gains comfort in his own self. It is an even, regular pulse, existing through time and space, organizing the horse not through frame but through breath. The regularity of the rhythm shapes the horse and puts him in mind of that all-important quality which is his responsibility in the partnership: self-carriage.

6. The precision of the rhythm leads to **flow**, our next ideal. From one pattern to the next, from one movement to the next in a seamless

manner, the transitions are effortless and evolving. There is no ceasing of the thought or the impulse behind them. Much like music, even the rests contain movement.

7. When we speak of **suppleness**, we are speaking in part of the ability of the horse to coil and recoil, (bascule), and ultimately set his haunches under him while raising his shoulders. It is suppleness that gives him both power and lightness, allowing energy to be generated and transformed into shape and movement.

8. **Compliance** is more than agreement and when considering the horse, indicates his receptivity to the rider's wishes. Horses are by nature receptive to their environment, constantly learning. Problems arise when a trainer doesn't know what or how much to expect from the horse or does not know how to ask. A compliant horse is one who is "on the aids," "in the hand," "in front of the leg," and "on the bit."

9. The next ideal in "Classical" dressage is **totality**, or the unification of the horse and rider. This is not merely a pretty picture but a mind-to-mind skeleton-to-skeleton merger of two disparate creatures who have come to exist on a common ground of mutual understanding. When this occurs, a third creature is given life: the horse/rider.

10. **Lightness**, our next ideal, is nothing more that the relative ease of communication between horse and rider. When hints rather than demands give rise to action, that is lightness. In a more narrow focus, lightness also refers to the mobility of the horse's shoulders because he has taken the predominance of the combined horse/rider weight onto his haunches.

11. **Moderation** is an expression of justice and as such, is a measure of the relationship between the rider and his horse. The temperamental display is not unleashed upon the horse when things go wrong but is subdued into understanding and perhaps questioning of the manner of the request. As the animal comprehends only two of the human emotions, love and fear, it is the practiced horseman who tempers his own thoughts and actions to comfort the horse rather than to make him fearful.

12. And last, but by no means least in our journey through the ideals of "Classical" dressage, is **virtue**. There is no doubt that the horse is a mirror of the person he is with and as such, reflects not merely the action of that person but more surprisingly, the intent. The evidence of virtue is the evidence of goodness, the upholding and practice of the "ideals of nature" without pretense or tyranny. Such should be the definition of morality.

Conclusion

When we deal with the "Classical" we are dealing with a vision of perfection. As daunting a prospect as that sounds, it is really no more than the selection and tempering of those qualities and ideals valued by all people for all time. In the study of philosophy and the arts, it is a given and a means of evaluating the permanence of a work or creator.

When dealing with the training and riding of the horse, however, we are tempted to evaluate his performance in terms of quantitative measures: How fast is he? How high can he jump? How accurate/handy is he? How strong is he? In this way we are measuring only the superficial aspects of the animal. "Classical" dressage, however, seeks if not to measure, then to elicit from the horse qualities that are not so readily seen. These are the interior nuances of the horse's being brought to the surface through mindful schooling and genuine partnership. The surface can be measured but only through adherence to the "ideals of nature" can the mysteries that are the horse be revealed.

WHAT IS CLASSICAL DRESSAGE?

How easy it is to judge a competition. Simply follow the rules and award a number based on how closely those rules are followed; a rather presumptive and naïve view of the living world, however.

But in the case of dressage, how do we judge those performances deemed "Classical?" Are they really so different from the typical competition performances?

In a word, yes. The intent of the Classical is a return to "the ideals of nature" as perceived by the ancient Greeks. As such, the ephemeral, the superficial, the display, have little to do with those qualities valued by Classical adherents. The Classical must not only be the best of its kind, but it must stand the test of time for all time. To accomplish that, it must suggest meaning: something more universal and resonant than mere appearance.

So what makes dressage "Classical?" Competitive adherents would have us believe there is no system of measurement and accuracy has little to do with the Classical but they would be wrong. For the criteria, however, we must look to the world of aesthetics rather than the world of science, utility, and sport. The work of a great sculptor, after all, is not judged in the same way as a soccer match!

The true Classical work goes leagues beyond what is competitive. In the Classical work we assume that the design is there: it is a given. It is the bones upon which the meaning or intent grows. Simply put, the structure of the Classical, the engineering of the work, is a prerequisite for its existence. It is the starting point from which departure should be inevitable and it is this departure which truly defines the depth of meaning of what is "Classical."

In dressage, likewise, there is craft and there is art. The craft is the exterior picture: how well is it done, does it follow easily grasped concepts, does it stay within the prescribed boundaries? The art, however, is embedded in those intangible qualities such as harmony, flow, grace, union, and totality, which make up the substance of the work. Not so easy to evaluate yet when these qualities are missing, the work is flat, one-dimensional. The resonance is gone; the breath is not given life. There is no intention which goes beyond the surface. No wonder then, the war between the Classical and competitive camps persists. There seems to be no common ground between them – except the horse.

There is no doubt that the horse is a reflection of the one he is with. As such, he manifests the intent of the rider whether it is in the spirit of sport or the spirit of beauty and here is the issue at odds: is the horse representative of a return to "the ideals of nature?"

The competitive horse obviously is not. He is subject to the artifice of sport and can only operate in the contortion and fixed position in which he is ridden, The ideal of self-carriage wherein the horse appears to be doing on his own what is asked of him is lost in the competitive arena. Nuance and intimate communication are nowhere in evidence. Instead, battles ensue between horse and rider with the horse begrudgingly maneuvered around an arena in endless, repetitive patterns. At this juncture, removing the rider would do little to enhance the picture since the horse has lost the ability to move in self-carriage in even so short a time as in the "giving of the reins."

In contrast, the classically trained horse draws attention to himself and away from the rider who all but "disappears" from the picture. He does seem to be acting on his own with the lightness of telepathy as his guide. He is not constrained and his gaits display the purity of the unencumbered horse. The bends within his body are continuous and equal in degree throughout. He shows no pockets of tension, only the increased energy of inspiration. In short, he is aware of his body in space and moves with an easy grace from back to front with lively haunches and light, mobile shoulders, carrying his rider with pride and enthusiasm.

This then is a word picture of the Classical horse, intrinsically and substantially different from the typical competitive horse. Can the two schools of thought ever reach an agreement even though they have the horse in common? Probably not. As the saying goes, "you ride the way you are" and until dressage is viewed not as sport, but as art and the rider as creator rather than athlete, there will be no consensus.

The horse is here to teach us something: who we are, where we fit within the world, how to live in mindfulness and grace. It would be a shame if we did not allow the horse to guide us on our return to "the ideals of nature."

MEDITATION FOR THE DRESSAGE RIDER

One of the alluring features of riding is the "alone" time it allows us away from the more prosaic concerns of life. It can be a breath of spring air, a sigh, an expansive moment in an otherwise hectic schedule. Riding can bring soft focus to our overloaded minds and a sense of nourishment to our bereft souls. It can rejuvenate with fresh meaning and renewed strength, repositioning our lives to open and receive.

But riding can also place us face-to-face with the unknown. It can remove us from the measurable and the compulsory which serve as guides in everyday life and deliver us to a far less tangible arena where the guideposts are dim or missing altogether.

For each rider, no matter what level of skill or experience has been attained, fear is a demon that darts in and out of our awareness. The horse flings his head up unexpectedly. We tighten. The horse stumbles. We tense and fall forward. In fact, the very act of climbing aboard the horse heightens our senses to a keen edge where we can tumble into the "no-zone" of panic.

What am I doing here? What happens if? Why is he doing that? Where am I going? Why can't I move?

All are reasonable questions to ask but fruitless from the back of the horse and even dangerous when stubbornly adhered to by the rider. To expect simple answers to questions such as these reduces riding to an uneasy formula and robs it of its very essence: the mutual understanding between two dissimilar creatures each in possession of a complete and unique perception of the world.

So what does meditation have to do with this "understanding" from our point of view as riders?

The act of meditation sends the mind to places not ordinarily visited in view of our propensity for logic. The logical mind is the stifled mind. It relies on categories and rules and hierarchal notions of good and bad, right and wrong. Logic, by definition, is obviously quite foreign to the horse though we do force him into the competitive arena and measure him against our artificial and sometimes arbitrary standards. The meditative mind, on the other hand, seeks truth above all. This is truth without any preconception about what that truth may turn out to be. It is open-ended. The meditative mind travels on its journey without end and without censor, merely allowing a continual creation of "what is."

Meditation then is all about the possible; not necessarily the probable, but the possible, and it is in this realm that we are privy to what is, not what we desire.

The object of meditation, (if there can even be said to be one), is to stop the mind's confused obsession with "little Me" and enter into the larger sense of "Me" as I am part of something greater and unknowable. The "little Me" vanishes as the mindful "Me" emerges, the "Me" that the horse recognizes as his true partner. It is, again, a "letting go" of the desire to control and an opening outward to the possibility that there is nothing to control but that the whole idea of control is an illusion. Beyond this illusion is the practice of meditation and the space it can provide us with for exploring not so much who we are as individuals, but who we are with the horse.

Meditation then, is a suppling of the mind, an act of continued thought centered on an idea without censure. The path taken by the ideal is left to the individual and is thereby unique and particular. The discovery is personal and infinite within that person, limited only by the inherent timidity of the seeker. There is no judge.

Inasmuch as meditation can be entered into anywhere and at any time, it is beneficial for us to make use of this freedom as often and in as many situations as possible. For our purposes, three distinct occasions emerge: away from the horse, in proximity to the horse, and on the horse. Obviously the nature of each will vary depending on the rider's whereabouts.

The following "embarking" ideas are meant as suggestions and need not be strictly adhered to. The journey is individual.

Away from the Horse

1. In a quiet, comfortable sitting spot, imagine you are telling your horse a story about your own inadequacies as a rider. You may begin with physical limitations, (gripping legs, unsteady hands), but should move on to more delicate and private matters suspected only by you.

- Do you demand instant obedience from you horse?
- Are you often frustrated by your horse's "horse nature" and his seeming indifference to your wishes?
- Do you believe a "hierarchy of intelligence" is relevant to you and your horse?
- Where do you place your horse in this "hierarchy?"

Now ask for your horse's help in overcoming these inadequacies. Apologize to him for specific indiscretions and again, ask for his help.

2. What is your horse without his body?

If you are stymied by this notion, think about personality, behavior, his presence or aura apart from any other living creature.

- What makes your horse who he is that no other creature is?
- Would you know your horse if you couldn't see him? How?
- Do either of you disappear when you are working together?

3. For this next meditation, the idea of "shape-shifting" will come into play. You will leave yourself and become your own horse talking with a candor particular only to animals.
- What self-knowledge would you wish to impart to your rider?
- What do you know that he only guesses at?
- How is your animal knowledge superior to his grasp of the world and what are you trying to teach him that he isn't quite comprehending?

In Proximity to the Horse

1. You want to catch your horse. As you walk toward the herd with halter in hand, you will one by one leave all "hunter" emotions behind. You are not a hunter aiming at a target; you are a seeker whose direction will be given by the horse. Observe his observation and become smaller, more open. Read his gestures and movement as the private incantations of an angel.
- Consider, what is awe? Are you in awe of your horse?
- Is awe an emotion of fear or of love?
- If you put fear and love on a scale, which outweighs the other in terms of how you feel about your horse?

2. You want to go into the stall with your horse. As you approach, you turn your thought to a religious space you have known; a church, a temple. You become quiet, hesitant, unsure of entry.
- How do you make yourself worthy of intruding upon this other world?
- How do you step, breathe?
- What do you say to your horse?

3. You admit to your desire for intimacy with your horse and wish he felt the same way about you. You want him to follow you but without a rein or a lead, he doesn't.
- What is it you are missing or what is it you should leave behind?
- You see him follow his herd mates and want to be with them. Why doesn't he want to be with you?
- How can you change yourself to be more like the horse he follows?

On the Horse

    1. You are tacked up and ready to mount. As you put your foot in the stirrup and bound upwards, you feel insecure, displaced. As you settle onto the back of the horse, ponder this question: Why, if you love to ride, are you afraid to ride?

Loosen your back, your legs, soften your hands.
    - Is it a nameless fear?
    - Can you put a name to it and send it on its way?
    Feel the connected horse; within himself, to you. Begin the silent conversation in humility and knowledge that you are exactly where you want to be.

    2. As you enter the arena before a show, clinic, lesson, etc., your busy mind is working overtime. What if you forget your test? What if the clinician doesn't like you? What if your teacher sees no improvement? You are in the fertile realm of pre-judgment and have even gone so far as to predict what others will say about you. Stop with your horse for a moment and consider why you are here.
    - If you leave your ego out of it, what else is there?
    - How do you want yourself and more importantly, your horse to be seen?
    - What is it that the two of you have together that no two others have?
    - Can you make the judge disappear?

    3. You have just started the young horse a week and a half ago and it is time for his first trot strides under saddle. "You know, you know, you know," you keep telling yourself for false courage but meanwhile you are sinking deep into the underbelly of fear and doubt. Halt and walk are fine but what will happen when you ask him to go forward?
    - Do you go forward in your life or do you carefully pick your way through the river preferring to see the stone clearly before you step on it?
    - Is your riding a metaphor for your life?
    - By changing your riding can you change your life?

As you urge your horse forward, open your chest. Expand and feel the fullness of the moment in your horse's unencumbered movement. Picture his acquiescence to your light aids, mere nuances that evaporate as soon as he senses them. You are in accord, moving on the same path with one impulse. It is so easy. This is what the horse will reveal.

Meditation then, is the trance of creation. It is the turning of a subject in the mind, exposing not only the pleasant but the uncomfortable aspects of that subject as well. It is the dimension of honesty where you are free to explore as you wish, in the precious "no-time" that is open and without obligation. It is a devotional act; to yourself, to your horse, to the "other" that is the both of you.

Meditation is a journey. Often labyrinthine, its goal cannot be predetermined and its result is often an experience of further wonder which, when brought back into the "real" world, softens and expands perceptions. When centered on the horse, the benefits are limitless since the horse himself is the great mediator, living as a unified whole, immune to the divisive personalities we wear.

On this journey, it is the horse and the mindful "Me," the "Horse/Me" that we meet again and again. It is as much the horse as it is the "Me," and further, the "Me" that is the horse and the horse that is the "Me." The lines of singular identity have been erased. Where one begins and the other ends is undetectable, unimportant. It is the new creation that resonates the balance and the harmony that is enough for a life; that is life.

GEOMETRY OF THE ARENA

Geometry is nothing more that the shaping of space. What was empty before and without form comes to life by the lines that surround it or the lines that move through it. Thus, the lines of the arena mark the finite space that is to be used while the horse and rider weave one geometric shape to another through movement. It is an arena of shapes within shape.

First and foremost, the arena is a grid. It can be divided by parallel lines, five in length and seven in width. Movements of the horse can then be directed along a course named by those lines and measured according to deviation from them. This is the arena as game board where scores can then be given for accuracy, i.e., where the movement started, where it ended, and whether it was executed within that space.

Since the arena is made of straight lines, it is also a reference for both straightness and bend in the horse. The horse is considered to be straight when his spine is parallel to the wall. The horse is considered to be bent when his body is paced at an angle to the fixed line and his spine is equally curved, dock to poll.

Within the rectangular arena then, all lines, angles, and bends are defined according to the fixed walls. Line denotes the track ridden. Angle defines the relationship of the horse to the wall. Bend measures the arrangement of the horse's body in equal degrees, back to front. And so, the shape of the horse is defined only in comparison to the fixed walls of the arena. It is obvious, however, that once the figures are learned absolutely, they can be done anywhere. After all, the twenty meter circle doesn't just mean going from "B" to "B" within the arena. It also indicates a certain bend within the horse's body and as such, can be created anywhere. The same holds true for all movements; the arena is simply a reference not for measuring distance outside the horse's body, but bend or straightness within it.

Next, the arena is actually a paradigm for the rider's body. The arena surrounds the horse in the same way that the rider's four walls (two hands and two legs) surround the horse. The "walls" the rider puts in place, however, are able to appear and disappear rapidly and are only individually active when the horse needs support in the posture of his body or the direction of his movement. Anyone who has done dressage in an open field knows that the horse is a consummate escape artist and like water, will flow through whatever door is open. Particularly when an outside aid is not attentive, the horse will seek to expand the arena on his own.

When we think of geometry, we think of a completed shape already in place. This is certainly true of the four rectangular walls of the arena. They do not move. But the horse and rider inside the arena do move in the creation of their geometry. All bends, turns, circles, arcs, spirals, boxes, and straight lines within the arena are traced stride by stride so that at any given time, only a fraction of the total shape is realized. Like any time art, however, the continuity is in the movement, not in the fixed form.

And so we have a beautiful paradox: the permanent surrounding, making a place for, and engendering the display of change through time. The geometry taking place is both solid and ephemeral, static and mobile. It is contained yet moving, earth under evolution. It is the permanence of change all in one space. It is life and nothing less.

GO FORWARD, BE ROUND

By nature, the horse behaves according to certain laws that affect the way in which he carries himself. When he is relaxed, at rest, or eating, he moves slowly or not at all with his topline stretching toward the ground. He is a model of energy conservation. When he is alert and stimulated, on the other hand, his body inverts with his head thrown high, his back hollow, and his hind legs out behind his mass in preparation for thrusting himself away from imminent danger. Both of these body positions are natural for the horse and are part of his "cellular knowledge," operating independently from our wishes or beliefs.

When we remove the horse from his "independent" posture, however, we must take into consideration his new burden: that of carrying a rider safely, soundly, and later, with as much individual expression as possible. For this, he needs a new "posture," one that elasticizes and softens his body and mind so we may enter and influence him. To achieve this, our repeated message, our mantra to the horse will be: "Go forward, be round. Go forward, be round." If we aren't telling him one, we are telling him the other. He is never without a message.

First comes "forward," then comes "round." Forward moves into round. Round receives forward. The actual time of execution: a fraction of a second. The horse can connect both of these elements from the very start of his training because the message never varies. This particular pairing avoids misunderstanding later on when we want to add one or the other to what is already habitual. Neither should be introduced by itself but as reciprocal halves of the same impulse. Round means forward, and forward means round. There is not one without the other.

If we think of the horse as a river flowing from back to front we can easily picture ourselves as both the banks of the river which changes direction and intensity, and the dam that filters the water going through it or stops it altogether. With rapid, light, and always terminal use of our legs, seat, weight, and hands, we can direct our river to be a rain-swelled gusher or a bubbling pool. It's all in the mix or proportion of the aids one to the other, measured in terms of intensity, duration, connection, timing of application, and timing of release. When appropriately given then, the aids induce the horse to go forward in such and such a manner.

Returning to the "forward and round" concept, it is not enough to do one without the other. The river must flow before it can be channeled; there is nothing to channel unless it flows. The two are absolutely indispensable to one another. "Forward" without round gives a careless, unintelligent, and often chaotic message to the horse. It also reinforces his alert posture:

emotionally tense, inverted, closed to the world of the rider. "Round" without "forward," while it may relax the horse, often anesthetizes him to the point of dullness and unresponsiveness. Again, he is closed to the world of the rider.

Simply stated, "go forward, be round" is not two distinct concepts to be taught separately to the horse, but two aspects of the same thing: energy. Create the energy; shape the energy. Feel the energy as it moves from the hind legs, up under your seat, and forward to your hands. This is the way it happens within the horse and in order for the rider to address that energy, (and here's the secret), there must be a slight separation of the aids, a time lag as long as it takes for the energy to travel from the back to the front of the horse. On a schooled horse, the application of the legs will immediately induce not only forward movement, but a rounding of the topline with the head and neck stretching toward the bit. On a less schooled horse the time between the two will be greater.

Though the goal is to achieve both "forward" and "round" at once in the picture of the horse, in truth, the requests from the rider are separated, quickly following one after the other. In other words, as the leg comes on, the fingers open; as the leg comes off, the fingers close. In effect, what we are doing is influencing the energy where it is at any given time in the horse's body, always touching for the onset of completion of a stride. By separating the aids we are shaping the horse not through concrete and unyielding walls but through the momentary appearance of the aids, showing the horse where to be, allowing the horse to become supple and malleable; to breathe in his work.

As the river flows forward, it does so in a particular shape, guided by the boundaries surrounding it; and so it is with the horse. He is enlivened and configured by our tactful aids which deliver the message: "Go forward, be round." In this world, there is always a place for him to be.

THE HALF-HALT

Of all that can be said of the half-halt, its primary purpose is to create and shape the energy of the horse. As such, it is a kind of recycling of that energy into form (or no form depending on its success). Since it addresses the continual creation of the horse from first to last stride, its use is also continual though intermittent. There is no one way to execute it, the manner dependent on what the horse has given and how it can be improved.

When the horse moves, his energy is created from his furthest backward extremity, his hind legs, moves forward over his back and neck, and ends at the furthest forward extremity, his head. The normal effect of adding energy to the horse results in two things: first, he will move his legs faster, and second, he will raise his head and neck, both a kind of stress response to the added energy. It is the job of the half-halt not only to address the position of the head and neck, but to connect it to the impulsion from behind (via the back) into a logical cause and effect relationship without the loss of that energy. It is a circular motion of creating the energy, shaping the energy without losing it, and returning it to its place of origin. In so doing, the horse stays in the center of his own balance.

The particular uses of the half-halt are many and varied. This is not to say that it is not also the primary means by which the rider stays in touch with the horse and keeps his attention. It is the essence of the mantra: "go forward, be round," gathering the horse together softly from back to front under the rider.

The stronger half-halt and the most frequently used is the "inside leg to outside hand" variety which is seldom used without harshness. It is employed as a kind of "alert" for what is to come, a preparation for a change of some kind as in the setup for a transition. In addition, the traditional half-halt is commonly used to regulate the speed of the horse and to reestablish a rhythm that has become irregular and without definition.

Over and above these obvious uses are more subtle ones which work toward the goal of self-carriage in the horse. The path to self-carriage often requires that the horse be rebalanced from front heavy to rear heavy. This is the essence of collection and by use of the half-halt, the hind legs become more engaged under the mass of the horse, and the shoulders become mobile and more elevated. If there is not a lighter and more effervescent feel in the hands after the half-halt, it was not successful.

Inasmuch as self-carriage is inextricably linked to lightness, the aids bear discussion as they pertain to the means for getting there. All aids act in one of two ways: they either support or suggest. Those that support are with the horse always and without them, he would come apart. They form a kind of mold into which the horse is driven and remain for the duration without major alteration. The aids that suggest, however, appear and disappear, allowing the horse some latitude for his own comprehension and adaptation to their demands. And so it is with the delivery of the half-halt.

So as not to stifle the movement of the horse, the half-halt is not delivered crudely or brusquely but with finesse and prior warning. In other words, the quality of the contact with the horse should be all that is needed with the half-halt taking on only slightly more emphasis than the normal touch of the leg or hand. Once the touches of leg (forward) and hand (round) have been lightly emphasized in firmness and duration, the horse should appear to glide forward as if a new sheen has been added to his movement. He should blossom.

If we use the "go forward, be round" mantra to explain how the half-halt works, it is easy to see that far from an erudite technique that is used only on rare occasions, it is actually a stride by stride possibility. If it works with the natural flow of energy and movement of the horse, it can actually become part of the fabric of communication with the horse; not a specialized tool. The half-halt most often employed, however, is far from multi-faceted and is used primarily for its power factor. If we tone it down a bit, however, and consider it a viable means of "keeping in touch" with the horse, here is what we have.

Right from the start we should understand that the message the half-halt delivers to the horse is threefold and thus cannot be dictated all at once. The complete message is:

"Get going…
In this manner…
Now do it yourself."

Realizing that this threefold message is consistent with the flow of the horse stride by stride goes a long way in feeling exactly how and when to do it. Note that the third phase of the message implies a total release of the aids, the phase at which we can ascertain just how close the horse is to self-carriage. It is his answer to the first two phases of the half-halt.

At its most basic, the half-halt works like this. (Singular "leg" and "hand" are used for the sake of simplicity.) The leg comes on and off and as the leg comes off, the hand closes in an upward direction and opens. These two actions comprise the first two directives to the horse: "Get going" (leg) and "In this manner" (hand). At this juncture, there is a release of the aids to allow the horse to respond. This is followed by the leg coming back on and so forth in a circular manner. It is of vital importance that neither hand nor leg is applied longer than necessary; shorter is better. It should also be stressed that the hand should never move back (retrograde to the motion) but always upward. This lifts the bit in the horse's mouth, points him toward lightness, and sends him on his way bypassing a confrontation where strength is used on both sides.

The half-halt then, is limitless when used to coincide with the horse's flow of energy, with his flow of movement. It is a pattern for each stride, a way of "keeping in touch" with the horse, and a way of subtracting from the barrage of aids we often succumb to using as riders. In short, the half-halt is a direct message from the rider to the horse to become both more powerful and ever lighter. Where else in life can these seemingly opposite qualities occur? Nowhere but in the self-carriage of the horse under you.

ONE-HANDED RIDING

There is always an inside rein and an outside rein. Generally, the inside attends to the shorter, more contracted side of the horse; the outside, the longer, stretched side. Even when the horse is moving straight, there is still a slight flexion to one side or the other due to the narrowness of the shoulders compared to the haunches. Each of the reins, therefore, has a different purpose and though they work in collaboration with one another, each rein necessarily must transmit and receive feel or message to and from the horse. This interchange via the reins does not vary simply because the reins are held in one hand. In principle, the transmission and reception are the same. The feel, however, is much less individuated.

To understand the role of the reins, we must know that they are the final aids to be used, always after and as a reflection of energy-producing seat and legs. As such, their primary purpose is to modify and shape the energy coming through the horse. They are always there, in position, connecting the horse to the hand, but they are not always active. In fact, there is a moment in each stride the horse takes when they are passive. This is when the hand receives from the horse the impact of his message back to the hand from which the hand then feels what its response should be. And nowhere is this felt more dramatically than when the reins are held in one hand.

One-handed riding therefore, localizes the feel of the horse in one place since the message is no longer traveling to two separate destinations. Centralizing the conduit of communication in this way reduces the "static" on the line and makes messages clearer and more direct. Once the rider is robbed of the ability to manipulate one rein against the other, several things happen: he no longer answers the horse with strength, and the horse becomes freer in his movement, both essential qualities of subtle communication between horse and rider. The conversations thus evolves through the nuances of position and vibration, rather than the force of steady insistence.

So all in one hand, each rein still has an integrity of its own and a distinct role to play depending on the desired shape of the horse. Objectively speaking, the inside rein bends, softens, and lightens the forehand of the horse. The outside rein guards, balances, rebalances, limits the outside shoulder and haunch, and stabilizes. The two reins together encapsulate the front third of the horse but also deal directly with the energy when it arrives there, keeping it along a course and turning the flow back to the haunches. In such a way, they work in quick collaboration with the legs to give efficient and expressive shape to the horse.

Subjectively, each rein also receives and transmits a message or "feel" to and from the mouth of the horse. Generally, the inside rein is the more playful of the two, constantly appearing and disappearing, commenting and allowing. Necessarily, the vibrations traveling through it are quicker and more animated. The outside rein, true to its objective function, is more stern, more firm, more "there" in maintaining a connection within the horse's body. Necessarily, the vibrations traveling through it are much slower and when timed with the footfalls of the horse, arrest the forward impulse and become the much lauded half-halts so widely discussed today.

So what does one-handed riding teach us? Primarily, it raises the rider's awareness of the other aids available with which to direct his horse. It takes away the emphasis on what is directly in front of his eyes and places the emphasis where it should be: throughout his entire body. In this diminished capacity, the hands can be used as they should be: as the quick punctuation to each thought or impulse of the horse or the rider, either finishing that thought or allowing it to proceed. The horse is therefore ridden with the seat, legs, torso, and weight, from back to front, with the hands merely modifying and shaping the energy as it travels through the latitude of the horse. The rider should feel the distinct separation of the aids as they work independently but follow one after the other, livening and shaping, livening and shaping until the horse becomes the reflection of the proportionate aids. One-handed riding can allow us this balance.

Riding *Sans* Stirrups

The legs lengthen to embrace. The seat opens to receive. The torso stretches both up from the waist and down from the waist. You are grounded, centered, without your feet firmly planted. You are riding without stirrups. If this description sounds too good to be true, it probably is.

Yours might read something like this: The legs shorten to clutch at the sides of the horse. The seat tightens to bounce ever higher as the trot gains momentum. The torso bends in the middle, contracting into a fetal position. You are flying, off-center, and you have no idea where your feet are. You are riding without stirrups (because you lost them long ago in the first walk-to-trot transition)!

Riding without stirrups is beneficial for the rider only if the latter description is simply an attempt at humor. If it is a reality, don't practice it. You will get better and better at being incorrect.

Riding without stirrups is not bareback riding, emulating the Cossack as he gallops along the Volga, or crouching low over the horse at a dead run to shoot a buffalo on the American plains. Riding without stirrups in the classical manner is an education in perfecting the double-headed concept of "least inference/most influence." In truth, this should be the quest of all serious riders and is the essence of the selfless though healthy "I." Not surprisingly, it is also the way to the horse.

Riding without stirrups has everything to do with lowering your weight into (not onto) the supple back of the horse. It is a kind of skeleton-to-skeleton depth of feeling, a connection between structures that are the basis of a newly created form. To accomplish this is not easy; it requires a number of conditions to exist simultaneously.

First, you should be able to adequately rotate your hip, knee, and ankle joints inward so that from the hip down, your legs lay flat around the barrel of the horse. This is contrary to the structure of most riders who find it easier to cultivate the *plié* position of classical ballet where the joints of the leg rotate outward. Unfortunately, this position forces the rider to ride off the back of his legs, tightens his contact, and deprives his leg of connection to the horse with as much surface as possible. In short, there should be no openings between any part of the legs and the sides of the horse, only a gentle hinged molding to his contour. This is the essence of the "breathing leg" which opens and closes with the horse as he moves and breathes. It is the allowing leg in constitution and the message-sending leg by virtue of its position on the horse.

Second, you should have complete control of you extremities so that your torso can be still. Without stillness, you cannot isolate and control specific body parts without others "following" along. The body then becomes noisy and the horse finds it impossible to detect any clear message so he tunes out, waiting until you sort out exactly what you want to say.

If we look at the horse as embodying the circular flow of energy from hind to fore and back to hind again, the necessity for the rider learning to isolate body parts becomes apparent. Without precise control of each of these parts, the flow takes random detours or is disconnected altogether. Control of body parts means isolating each part to learn where it is in space and more importantly, how to reach it through your mind. Only after this rather lengthy process has taken place can the newly awakened and enlivened parts be strung together again to form a coordinated whole.

Next, you should be able to locate your center of gravity between your lower back and lower abdomen and give it existence with deep, slow, diaphragmatic breathing. This is your core and the lower it is, the closer you are to the horse. Your center of gravity is the same as your point of balance and, influenced by the movement of the horse, is in constant flux. Balance is not static but ever adapting, shifting to accommodate new needs brought on through movement. Within a single stride, the internal adjustments made by the rider are countless and riding without stirrups puts the rider closer to this necessity. The single most important property of the rider's balance is that it is in fact never apprehended and dismissed. It is the embodiment of change, of adjustment, of being in the moment.

Fourth, in order to ride effectively without stirrups, the rider needs to learn both theoretically and viscerally the six dimensions of the horse's movement: back to front, up to down, and side to side. In the beginning, this can seem like chaos but it has both rhyme and reason to it.

Any given moment in a horse's stride can be measured in dimension. In other words, it exists within limitations. For example, the horse only goes so far back in the canter depart and only so far forward in it. In that same canter depart, he also moves from outside to inside and from up to down, both within limits. It is the task of the rider to first be able to follow these "dimensions" without impeding them by learning what is going on underneath himself at any given moment. It is only after he has a thorough knowledge through feel that he can begin to augment or diminish the dimension of each stride in any of six directions. The mental decision to alter or leave alone comes only after the rider's complete body awareness is an afterthought.

And finally and most importantly, the foundation on which all of the physical is built is this: that the rider has consciously given himself up to the horse with not even a flicker of doubt as to where he wants to be. He is not performing mental isometrics on himself by saying "yes" but demonstrating "no." In other words, he has integrated his mind and body to agree with one another: right thought, right action. For this, the mind must be quiet and controlled, steady and deliberately in place with each movement of the horse. Only then can the rider make the necessary changes in his body.

Riding without stirrups is all about mastering the tension within the body and within the mind. Which comes first is not possible to say but it is possible to say that the body can be quieted by the mind's focused insistence, and the mind can be quieted through the body's cultivated response. Both in turn can then find serenity within a deeper connection to the horse.

A Good Conversation

It is difficult to remember when the handwritten letter was a measure of the cultivated mind, dance was an elegant expression of intimacy between two people, and conversation was imbued with respect for what was being said. Those times appear to be long gone. Courteous exchange has been replaced by the despotic assertion of "I" and "I" hates to listen. When he does, he feels open, vulnerable; not at all the most enviable of positions to be in. But substitute the word "receptive" for "vulnerable" and the idea seems not at all bad, even somewhat admirable.

In the deliverance of the aids, it is precisely the open, "receptive" position that is most often neglected. (It is the one that holds our fear.) The usual application of the aids goes something like this: the hands are closed, the legs are activated, the horse reacts, the rider maintains the aids thinking, "I've got the response I wanted so I must maintain my aids in the same manner to keep that response."

This is erroneous thinking. This is what gives our horses cramped, stiff movement and makes them an unpleasant ride. There is no conversation going on here, only a one way speech given by the rider. It's no wonder horses "tune out," take a vacation, send their minds to greener pastures. We really are giving them the impression that we don't value what they think or feel and whatever way they react, our response is always the same: Maintain the aids.

If we take apart a good conversation and examine how it operates, we find that it has a very definite structure, one that allows for the circulation and refinement of ideas between two parties. It is not a one-way harangue. It is a living, breathing exchange with the effort always toward mutual agreement. The energy never stops or congeals within one party but belongs to both and as such, is sent freely back and forth.

Within the tenth of a second or so that it takes for an interchange between horse and rider to occur, three things should happen:

- The message is given to the horse (the rider waits),
- The horse responds (the rider assesses),
- The rider responds (to the horse's action).

It is a self a self-perpetuating structure, a circular flow of communication that should repeat itself over and over again whenever we enter into a conversation with the horse. If any of these steps is neglected, the circle is broken with both parties talking at once, neither listening. Communication is lost and more than likely it is the rider who descends to the role of autocrat endlessly barraging his horse with the chatter of his stronger and stronger aids. Unfortunately, this is an all too common occurrence and though a small percentage of horses will go along with the overkill of the aids, a larger number will either fight or leave, at least mentally.

So in practice, how does this equitable association work? The first step is for the rider to initiate the conversation. It could be as simple a message as "walk on from the halt," or as difficult as "passage from the rein-back." Whatever the message, the crucial part of step one follows quickly after the request: wait. That's right. Do nothing. Remember that in a conversation it is precisely the alternation between two parties that gives it its definition. Without waiting, how can you hear what the other party is saying? More to the point for our purposes, without waiting, how do you know if the horse is attempting to respond or not?

During the time the rider waits for the horse's response, the aids do not maintain or re-demand, but become passive to allow the response. This is the most difficult moment for the rider as he has to do nothing. He must refrain from further comment on what he has already asked until he has heard from the horse.

Once the horse responds, (step two), the response is quickly assessed by the rider. Does the action of the horse require a correction? If so, where? Does it require an affirmation? If so, how?

Here, the correct judgment of the rider is critical to the furtherance of the horse's willingness. If the rider is not just, (even bordering on the brink of generosity), the horse will either shut down or escape and the rider will have to rethink his original assessment. Fortunately, the rider's brain can be quickened through practice. There is no time for deliberation here. The brain must operate as a reflex if the horse is to understand.

Once the decision has been made, the aids are quickly brought into play, (step three), and say the same thing to the horse as the brain (picture) has just formulated. This is the point at which some talented riders have claimed telepathy at work. When the brain (judgment) and body (action) are in such a purposeful agreement, why shouldn't the receptive horse pick up on a mental image even before it is reiterated through the physical aids? Perhaps this is the very essence of self-carriage in the horse; manifesting the physical through the mental. As there is no separation within the horse between the mental and the physical, so should there be no separation within the rider. The integrity of the conversation depends on it.

As much as the horse is a reflection of what the rider says to him and is prevailed upon through the rider's thoughtful guidance, he is also the keeper and arbiter of the language of this conversation. It is through his movement that the rider first is made aware of the language, second, learns it, and third, spends a lifetime refining it. To enter into a conversation with such a partner demands complete clarity of intent and clarity of deliverance. The horse has a predilection for being mute and unresponsive when clarity is obscured.

Taking apart the living structure of a good conversation can be a futile endeavor. Often, before the words are even uttered, the topic has changed. The key here, however, is the rider's determination to wait for the statement of the horse before he himself responds. Smaller sentences help; focus and discipline are crucial. Without the wait when the rider does nothing, the horse will cease to be a conversationalist himself and will descend to the role of obedient slave, offering nothing of his own unique self.

Conversation is a dynamic exchange. It can be the very expression of courtesy and respect, or it can disintegrate to a tiresome speech of one. How it goes depends upon the rider. After all, the horse is waiting.

Movement

"This horse knows all the movements up through Prix St. Georges," says the high, sing-song voice from the twentieth century.

"Yes, but this horse has elegant, collected movement," says the low, deep voice from the eighteenth century.

"But he doesn't do the skips," whines the modern voice again.

"And I'm certain, my dear, that yours has never even heard of a pesade, let alone a levade, gallopade, croupade, or passade," responds the slightly glib voice.

And so, a controversy is born.

When we describe the horse, there is both "movement" and "movements."

"Movement" denotes the substance and quality of the three gaits. As such, it represents a kind of signature of the individual horse, infinite in possibility. "Movements," on the other hand, refers to the positions and gymnastic exercises we practice to improve the quality of the gaits. They are the means to an end, finite in number and beneficial only insofar as they remain on the track of creating individual expression. If the movements do not lead to an improvement in the horse's gaits, it is not dressage. Therefore, the pirouette improves the canter; the piaffe improves the trot. It is not the other way around.

The Old Masters advocated quite a different progression in the schooling of their horses than is currently understood. First off, the canter was not seriously practiced until the piaffe was well underway. The idea here was that balance in the horse was to be established before he was asked to negotiate the asymmetrical qualities of the canter. The result? By all accounts, the horse was immediately able to canter straight and move into the counter canter and pirouette without the necessity of interminable correction because the gait had been practiced for so long in a state of imbalance. Once balance was achieved, the gait itself was no problem for the horse.

Next, the Old Masters believed that the primary goal of schooling the horse was to collect him. Therefore, what we define as medium and extended gaits were unknown to them. They would have been scandalized to even consider "lengthening" the horse before collection was established. He was already in the naturally long and unwieldy shape making it impossible for him to be the powerful, agile mount they so desired. So, collection was not only the goal but the wellspring from which all else flowed.

The first rule of the Old Masters was: if it doesn't improve the gaits, it is not useful in the schooling of the horse. Thus, what we term the canter changes "a tempi" were not practiced and in particular, the changes every stride, (or what is familiarly known as "skipping"), would have been looked upon as a grotesque distortion of the canter gait itself. The single changes were employed but in and of themselves, were not given nearly the importance we attach to them today.

And finally, the Old Masters were great observers and quickly discarded from their program of training, any practice which would reinforce the horse's natural inclination to be crooked. Thus, the travers was used initially but once the horse understood the movement, was replaced by the renvers which put the haunches in the opposite position from where the horse wanted to carry them with no correction. The emphasis on the renvers, (and by inference, the counter positions), was what imparted to the horse the quick flexibility of body and mind so prized by the Old Masters. From this perspective, we can see that they adhered to the laws of nature and departed from them only when it aided in the creation of a powerful, balanced, and agile riding horse.

When thinking of the movements then, it is essential that we understand the dimensions of the horse's gaits. He can move: forward or backward, left or right, bent or straight, on or off the ground, and in collected, school, working, medium, and extended gaits. These are the primary positions affected by practice of the movements. Within these limitations of movement, we have created the movements per se which include: the three basic gaits and their variations, the lateral movements, turns on the forehand, haunches, and center, the counter canter, the flying changes of lead, and the more specialized piaffe, passage, and airs both on and above the ground. Each of these movements has a role to pay in sustaining the purity and increasing the expression of the gaits.

The Old Masters would have described their fully trained horse with adjectives like fluid, powerful, agile, graceful, and harmonious. They would have eschewed a list of movements the horse could perform in favor of offering a picture of how he moved. It was movement, after all, that distinguished the pedestrian from the refined.

The movements themselves then, are designed to amplify the horse's suppleness, strength, and brilliance. Their use is limited only by the ingenuity of the trainer. The quality of movement, however, depends on the expertise of the artist. The two together induce and allow the horse both connection and freedom, the two seemingly opposite ingredients necessary for him to fulfill his promise as a ridden horse and to become an inspiration for achieving elegance of movement.

Observations from Work in-Hand

In the classical training of the dressage horse, there is a progressive intimacy that evolves not merely through association over time, but also through proximity in space. The distance between horse and human has a profound effect on how well and in what detail the two listen to one another. The further apart, the more likely sensitive messages become diluted and lose their original intent. The closer together, however, the greater the possibility for refinement of communication through an uninterrupted dialogue.

Of the three traditions of working the horse from the ground — lungeing, long lining, and work in-hand—it is work in-hand that fosters the kind of intimacy closest to mounted work. While lungeing allows the partners an opportunity for studying one another and setting down the rudiments of communication, it still outlines the horse and human as distant creatures. The practice of long-lining shrinks the space between the two but emphasizes the rein-heavy, driving, psychology so harmful to true intimacy. It is the work in-hand then, that choreographs the dance between the horse and human in its most refined shape, without the physical effort so often displayed during mounted work. It can be the ultimate in nearly invisible interchange.

The benefits to be gained from work in-hand are countless for both horse and trainer. From the very beginning of the horse's education up to the high school, work in-hand can be used to introduce and later to refine the responses of both partners into a seamless dialogue. Both become "tuned in" and intent on their work without the distractions likely through greater distance between the two, or through the inadvertent and sometimes unavoidable clumsiness of the rider when mounted. Work in-hand is the "tete-a-tete" of the horse/human relationship where proximity gives rise to a courteous exchange of ideas between two interested partners. It is a meeting of the minds, a private, agreeable, face-to-face chat.

Whereas lungeing teaches the horse to go forward, it is work in-hand that teaches the horse to come back to the trainer. It is the trainer's world into which the horse is invited and the one in which he is expected to perform, much like the induction of a child into the world of adults. In this world there is a code of behavior that must be followed by both parties.

The world of work in-hand is a very small one, literally, one in which steps can be measured. Because of its exacting nature, it is as if both horse and handler are put under a microscope where the slightest response of either is suddenly amplified to a degree which becomes more significant than the response itself. For both creatures, work in-hand is a barometer for the real nature of their relationship.

Undoubtedly, one of the advantages of incorporating work in-hand into the training program is that the horse can begin learning the vocabulary of schooling much earlier in his life, quite some time before he is physically able to be ridden. The "shaping" process is far easier to introduce to the horse without the burden of the rider and can proceed at whatever rate the young horse is able to accept. Most often, the young horse is far more capable in his mind than we give him credit for; he learns from the moment he enters the world. The work in-hand is a soft work that may be tailored to challenge his eager, inquisitive mind and instill a code of acceptable behavior but present no harm to his developing body.

Beginning as well as advanced work in-hand should immediately bring the horse into the trainer's world. What this actually means is that the horse is in the "on the bit" position from where he is reachable and able to be influenced. The benefits for his body are great: stretched topline, raised back, flexion in his poll and jaw, increased activity of his haunches, and unity of movement. The benefits for his mind are immeasurable, particularly those of calmness and concentration.

The "on the bit" position or the connection between the mouth of the horse and the trainer's hand, is a focal point of the work in-hand. Rather than driving up to the bit, the horse can be softly put together through sideways or straight movement, and by lowering and stretching his head and neck. The advantage for the trainer of being on the ground when asking the horse to yield in the poll and jaw is that the hand has two more available directions to explore: down and forward, obviously not available when on the back of the horse. What this offers the trainer is a more complete palette of sensations to suggest to the horse. Exploration in this soft and relaxed manner usually leads quickly to the onset of dialogue.

So for the horse, the work in-hand offers advancement without stress, in essence, lightness in carriage within boundary. It is the best of all possible worlds. It is the means for making the horse soft without him learning to be strong against the method or person behind the method. Correct work in-hand is thus a means of real training, not mere conditioning or habituation of the horse to a deadly everyday routine. If the trainer understands the concepts the horse needs to learn, the work in-hand is a treasure. All foundations exist within it and all possibilities arise from it.

For the trainer of the horse, work in-hand is no less beneficial and has one advantage over riding: the trainer can see the whole horse, back to front, bottom to top. This can be invaluable when checking on the validity of what he can only feel when riding and can increase his sensory acuity which he can then take back to the saddle knowing more precisely what the "feel" looks like.

When the head of the horse is as close to the trainer as would be his favorite dance partner's, certain perceptions are likely to arise. First and foremost is that the working of the hands will be magnified because that working is so directly given to the horse and his response is in turn so direct. Small escapes like the rolling of an eye to the outside of the arena can actually be felt in the hand and quickly redirected back to the inside. Nowhere is the necessity of the outside rein felt more dramatically than when the trainer can see it fluctuating between a boundary and an open door. And nowhere can the potentially ruinous inside hand be so pronounced as it is when it is right in front of the trainer's head. Bad, bad hand must learn not to be so serious! Not surprising is that the work in-hand is just that: the shaping of the live clay in front of you with pats and presses and sweeps of the fingers while the eye persistently evaluates the evolving work. For precision of eye, there is no better instructor than the sensitive hand. And conversely, for the cultivation of the hand, the eye can never be too acute.

To be in tune with the horse means being in step with him, not merely in the same space but in the same time as well. There is nothing more disjointed than the horse and human parading around the arena, each listening to a different tune! There is no unity; there is no purpose. And the trainer bears sole responsibility for this for once again, it is his world he is bringing the horse into. For this he must let no perception of the horse escape, even if his own shortcomings doubt the abilities of the horse to be totally captivated. It is the perception of rhythm as it relates to step and rhythm as it relates to breath that is one of these unexplored areas.

Make no mistake, steady rhythm is essential to the horse's ease and comfort for it is an indication of regular breath. Not only in the tasks we give him to perform, but also in his quite extensive time apart from us, a steady and predictable rhythm signifies not only a well-oiled body, but a mind and psychology at ease with the environment. And likewise does the horse perceive us to be serene or agitated by the rhythm of our step and breath.

For the trainer, the delicate quality of the work in-hand offers the perfect opportunity for tuning the horse in to recognition of nuance within his body and by extension, capability in reading the intent of his mind. In the work in-hand, it is the trainer's job to convince the horse that indeed, the trainer's mind, (at least the part he allows the horse access to), is focused, intent, undisturbed, peaceful, just like the mind of the horse in steady rhythm. In short, it can be readable and more to the point, it is recognizable. To be recognized by the horse, in both senses of the word, ("who" in terms of identity and "what" in terms of consistence), is the trainer's ultimate measure of success. It in only then that he can begin to influence and expand the horse as he so deserves.

Through the work in-hand, the foot dance between horse and trainer, each is known to the other through common ground. It is there that the basics of the relationship are laid out, raised to performance, and set spinning between the two. Work in-hand is nothing less that the act of knowledgeable intimacy and palpable trust.

Shape-Shifting

Throughout the ages, people have explored the mystery of transformation. Deep in forests, in caves, in houses of worship, they have gathered to witness and to practice this ancient art. The idea of becoming something other than what we are has held great fascination for the seekers among us and has been the subject of countless folk tales, legends, and even religions. From the Greek god Zeus changing to a flea to further his amorous pursuits to King Arthur becoming a fish to gain wisdom, the lure of escaping the present body in favor of another has infused our history with a sense of longing, restlessness, and escape; all undeniably human characteristics. Even popular culture offers up Batman and the Werewolf as archetypal transformation figures.

Perhaps the first metamorphosis was observed in the natural world: the polliwog became the frog, the caterpillar became the butterfly. Both grew into creatures more capable than they started out. The polliwog was no longer confined to water but sprouted legs and crawled onto land. The caterpillar no longer inched along on a branch but grew wings and soared above his humble origins.

In all transformation stories, the change brings betterment. In the case of human transformation, the wish is to become an animal: to possess those qualities that as humans, we lack. We rise in power and status by virtue of our new animal demeanor. (How odd that we place ourselves at the top of the "food chain" when secretly we wish to be more like what we eat!)

Be that as it may, we have looked at animals enviously, coveting what we perceive to be their superior attributes and adopting those behaviors we deem particularly alluring or useful to us. We always come back, however, hoping to bring into our human form what we have learned from the animals.

The attributes of particular animals are also worthy of emulation when dealing with horses. (When seeking to influence an animal, learn from another one.) It is for this reason that the practice of shape-shifting, or temporary transformation, can add new dimension to the vocabulary of training.

Shape-shifting is an actor's tool. It requires that the actor leave himself for a time and become someone or something else complete with the mental, psychological, and even physical attributes of that "shape" he is entering. The more thoroughly he is able to adopt his new guise, the more convincing is his portrayal. When attempting to impress a horse, the strength of the persona becomes even more important.

The value of shape-shifting for the trainer is that he temporarily leaves behind his own shortcomings and becomes something else of a simpler yet more potent quality. This is quite readily understood by the horse since it is a complete message with no room for misinterpretation. It is a mask, but one of which the horse is unaware.

Much as the Greek gods were endowed with human qualities which were exaggerated to fit their positions as gods, we are going to choose three animals who possess singular strengths and use these strengths in our dealings with horses. While each of us may possess these strengths in part or at various times, it is the absolute and complete animal we are trying to learn from, the essence of which is pure and unalterable. He is what he is, undiluted, complete. His identity is him and he is his identity, without conceit.

The Lion, the Gnat, and the Turtle

Far too often the problems we encounter with the horse occur when we ignore the fundamental requirement that he knows where he stands in relation to us. This is not a training problem per se, but it does influence every single encounter and an imbalance in this understanding can escalate to the point where all communication is lost. The relationship backslides to a series of skirmishes, "tests," if you will, which we fail miserably. The horse needs a position to be able to negotiate his world. If he is confused about where he belongs, he will continue to seek his own role as leader in that partnership. It is a rigid hierarchy to which he belongs, one governed by the instincts of the prey animal.

By contrast, the predator, the mountain lion, is a solitary animal, the seeming "master of all he surveys." He is quick and lethal with a non-negotiating edge. It is his way or none at all and it is precisely this aura of superiority we can learn from him and "put on" when dealing with our horses. Whether or not we actually believe or feel the superiority in an intellectual or internal way doesn't matter. What matters to the horse is that we are convincing and our ability to become the actor in the guise of the mountain lion is what he perceives.

The message should be clear: "I am leader. I am number one, you are not. This is not open to discussion. You will do as I say." If this seems harsh, remember that the horse is accustomed to receiving and obeying messages such as this from members of his own species. This is a large part of the way in which his society maintains its cohesiveness, its order. Without threat and deliverance if necessary, the society of the horse would crumble. Without a leader, it would fall into chaos, an easy target for the mountain lion.

As the lion, it's your opportunity to lower the horse to subordinate. This is never a constant but much like what occurs in nature, you make your presence known, make the change, and vanish. The lion in no way maintains, only influences. He is quick and single-minded. There is no doubt in his intention or his movement. He is a unit of form and content, each supporting the other.

As the lion, you will become omnipotent. Your body will rise, expand, and encompass the horse. Your thought will be unwavering. Whether working from the ground or the saddle, the horse must never suspect that you are not really the mountain lion ready to strike and lay bare his bones if need be. He must be convinced. You must be both convinced and convincing.

The mountain lion guise is particularly useful when introducing young horses to what is expected of them or for re-schooling the older horse who is reluctant or unresponsive. He demands three things from the horse: "Go forward now. Stop now. Put your head down now." In short, the mountain lion orders his space and accepts nothing less than complete acquiescence. Once the desired reaction is achieved, usually in only a matter of moments, he fades to become the quiet observer: the well-fed cat.

The mountain lion's gift to us is the gift of clarity; of a single statement uttered with great precision and direction which cannot be ignored or misunderstood. It is the imperative. The intensity of the statement is not more than is needed but is sufficient in response to the horse, to effect change; slightly more than what the horse offers.

Among our animal "role models," the mountain lion is only part of the shape and tone we need to acquire in order to make the horse fully understand our wishes. The tiny gnat is also worth of study and emulation, not for his threatening visage, but certainly for his pointedly focused life. The gnat, as well as other members of the insect world, is tireless. His life allows for no distraction. Though diminutive in a world of giants, he is striking in his ability to get what he wants through sheer persistence.

By contrast, the rider vacillates. First he wants the head and neck of the horse long and low. Then he wants the horse up in front. Then come the gadgets, the "fixing:" the change of bits, the heinous "head-set," and finally, for lack of a better solution, abandonment altogether in favor of one of the countless methods of "natural horsemanship." The saintly and long-suffering horse, if not utterly confused, has by now certainly adopted an air of resignation and impenetrability, if not downright rebellion.

The gnat would never have engendered such a reaction from another creature. The gnat is not about confusion; his entire life is one of discipline. His discipline is possible because he has a clear knowledge of what he wants. If we are to become the gnat, this puts the singular burden of knowing what we want from the horse directly on us. We have to know what is correct: what it looks like, what it feels like, how to make those million modifications while in motion to keep the picture always the object of our actions. If we waver, all is lost and direction becomes arbitrary. The picture disintegrates into unconnected detail: scraps and wishes. The gnat unifies the horse, gathers him together and makes him aware of his body in space.

The gnat's message to the horse is one of decisiveness. He is quick, nagging if need be. "I am correct in the aids I am delivering and I am prepared to 'bug' you all day until you acknowledge me." With persistence like that, how could the horse refuse? One is reminded of Baucher's "effet d'ensemble" of the first manner in which the horse is alternately told to activate the haunches and to yield in the jaw in rapid succession. On the spot the horse is asked to gather himself together, first one end, then the other, much as the "attack" a gnat would initiate. What undisputed influence from an almost unseen force. This should be considered in connection with the "invisible" aids we all desire.

If the gnat is the embodiment of the quick and insistent message and the mountain lion the voice of authority, our next animal model provides the qualities by which these two are balanced. The turtle has long been associated with the very idea of balance and has even been given the attribution, by some cultures, of carrying the world on his back. What a worthy and steadfast creature to emulate in our training of the horse.

The demeanor of the turtle is calm, slow, and deliberate. He takes time and rolls it out before him on an endless carpet of serenity, seemingly indifferent to the distractions surrounding him. He is the personification of soft, all encompassing focus, gently making his way through life with a grace impervious to the ups and downs of the more dramatic animals. (If the mountain lion is the full-throated roar and the gnat the high-pitched soprano, certainly the turtle is the consistent drone over which the other two resound.) He is the "good guy," secure in the knowledge of his place in the scheme of things and content to be just that: the foundation upon which frequent and subtle change is grounded.

For the trainer of the horse, the turtle becomes a guide when we have mastered ourselves to the degree that we are in control of our bodies and emotions. This, or course, presupposes that our attitudes toward the horse have already been finely honed, perfected to the degree that they allow the turtle to teach us. When the turtle speaks, he speaks softly. What he says, he says often but in plain language. "I am asking you to go. I will not get in your way. I am with you."

The turtle then, inspires confidence in those he touches. He is physically slow and deliberate, almost telegraphing beforehand what his next action will be. His mind is calm, perceiving his world in time with each new step. No wonder the turtle is comprehensible to the horse. He lives in the "now" while going forward in an undeviating tempo. The horse gains comfort from this regularity and can then express himself, knowing that the turtle is always there.

When considering the application of the aids, the turtle becomes an even more interesting subject for study and emulation. While the turtle is nothing if not dependable, he also possesses the ability to disappear at will by retreating back into his shell. This "vanishing act" is a great gift to the rider struggling with the notion of the horse's self-carriage and self-impulsion. The rider must learn that in order for the horse to "do it himself," the rider must disappear, and disappear often. The turtle's message is: "Now I'm here, now I'm not. Do it yourself. If you need help, I'm here, but only for an instant." What wonderful restraint is displayed by the turtle, the foundation on which the world is carried.

The act of shape-shifting then, is the act of transformation, the nature of which is quick, miraculous. It is evidence of understanding, the spark of insight that comes from temporarily escaping the barriers or human-ness and allowing the non-human voice and skin to amplify our limited and predictable actions. It is going out of the self for a special knowledge that can only be acquired out of the self and returning more fully cognizant than before of the nuances of inter-connectedness.

Much as the shaman enters worlds that are not himself to gain the wisdom that cannot be gained while in his traditional guise, so should the person seeking greater understanding of the horse enter into animal awareness and behaviors which will sensitize him to perception that is not his own. Apart from the possible benefits to the individual in areas other than communication with the horse, it is entirely necessary to perceive with other eyes, other skin, in order to even begin a conversation of mutual respect. It is the least we can do to offer the horse a more open hand, one which senses as he does, and the most we can do for ourselves, to gain a sense of the horse as he is, not as some product of our delusions. What we are able to gain from the lion, the gnat, the turtle, we are unable to learn from anyone else. These creatures are specialists at being themselves and no one can do it better. What they possess and offer willingly, we lack and suffer in incompleteness. The might of the lion, the persistence of the gnat, the steadfastness of the turtle are all qualities we can "put on" our exteriors, and allow to permeate our depths as we become more like the horse in his entirety.

What the horse understands is not simple, but profound. What the person understands, he energetically tries to make simple. He misses entirely the truth that what appears on the surface to be simple is "simply" symptomatic of the larger world underneath where the word loses its necessity and the unambiguous communication begins: the roar, the buzz, the drone. It is through mastery of these voices that the horse recognizes the familiar dimension of his own world, a world to which we have been led softly and patiently by the others who speak without words.

Letting Go

Increasingly, it seems that it is the act of "letting go" that defines and qualifies our relationships with our horses.

On first awareness, "letting go" is often inspired by simply looking at the horse as he cavorts freely around his paddock or assumes a statuesque profile listening to distant rumblings. We give ourselves over to his magnificence and lose ourselves in the moment. He is another being, apart, that we wish to come close to; an attraction not unlike the initial stirrings of a love affair. The prospect is at once so consuming, that we abandon all recognition of our overly potent selves in order not to disturb that delicate image we have of unmatched harmony with this beloved beast. If we can just return to that initial inspiration, that first ecstatic high, we will have reached perfection.

But alas, there is more to art, heaven, and the horse/human relationship than inspiration. The quality we desire requires a conscious decision to allow the horse to participate in the partnership with as little interference from us as possible. In its cultivated state, "letting go" necessitates a scrupulous fidelity to our initial inspiration which is, after all, what drew us to the horse in the first place. Retrieving that first blush of euphoria is not simply a matter of waiting but of "letting go" repeatedly of whatever perverts that sacred union with the horse.

The practice of "letting go:" is both physical and mental. It begins away from the horse with a deliberate discarding of those thoughts and impulses which get in the way and undermine our goal of "the allowing." If it does not send us forward in soft eagerness, we don't need it. We must let it go. In fact, everything we think we know, everything we rely on, everything that gives us a sense of security or permanence should be exiled to the distant past. In place of these distractions, we will put four concepts which will become reflex practices, as easy as breathing. They are: benevolent intention, the heart/mind/hand reflex, the absence of past and future, and the non-judgmental mind. The attainment even in small measure of any of these practices will place us exactly where we should be: in a state amenable to receiving from the horse his shy understanding and the great gift of his "tender comradeship."

The first replacement concept relies on a deceptively simple notion: that fundamentally, we wish to do no harm even though we know that existence itself may contradict that wish. It depends on our ability to tread lightly and to restrain a strong will that would seek to overpower rather than to abide with.

"Benevolent intention," then, is the wellspring from which all noble action arises. It is a constant and unlimited source of inspiration to which we will return again and again. It is a giving up of all but our most compassionate thoughts and actions, remembering always the purity of our first attraction.

In reality, "benevolent intention" is a kind of surrender. Much as we expect our horses to give up their instincts, bodies, and minds, we too have a requirement: that we shed those incomprehensible human actions done out of frustration, anger, and false supremacy. When we meet the horse, he will recognize us by the honesty and selflessness with which we extend a hand. It is our entire strength in this relationship.

The second concept, the "mind/heart/hand reflex," is a technique of integration, bringing all disparate tendencies of the human into accord. Whether its genesis comes about through a conscious decision to improve, an overpowering emotion, or a physical feeling of imbalance, it makes little difference. It is the practice of the "mind/heart/hand reflex" that unifies us within ourselves and allows us to be in balance with the horse. Fractured as we commonly are, it is the horse who can make us whole. He can suggest our very breathing, if we allow; it is that easy, it is that fundamental. Openness to change is the key; rigidity is the closed door.

Beginning with the mind, we can make the decisions to be flexible, to be allowing. The horse's actions are simply the horse's actions, neither good nor bad. Our place within his world is what we wish to explore, not the "supremacy" of the human intelligence. We are watching the horse with impartiality and lively curiosity. What can he teach us? What can he tell us about ourselves?

As soon as the mind rests in open spaces of possibility, the heart is allowed its way, usually with an honesty and sense of purpose unequaled in the human to human relationship. The heart speaks with the passion of unknowing and is comfortable. The heart speaks with the courage of desire and knows it is right. The heart guides the rider in goodness, the mind in justice.

With the mind and heart unified in quiet acquiescence, the hand can follow in like manner. The all-important release of the hand is no longer an impossibility. It is now the physical illustration of our open minds and hearts, allowing the free flow of current, energy, information, to pass uninhibited between us and the horse.

The "mind/heart/hand reflex," however, is far more than a dogmatic formula for the dysfunctional rider. It is nothing less than a way of existing, a state of being, that is understandable, comfortable, and non-threatening to the horse. It is, quite possibly, a duplication in some measure of the way in which the horse exists. And even further, perhaps the "mind/heart/hand reflex" is a structure that exists in all of nature: thought, (awareness), then feeling, (perception of a more immediate and personal variety), then physical action.

At the very least, the acquisition of some semblance of harmony within us as riders before we intend to communicate with the horse, is an idea not without merit. At the very most, the "mind/heart/hand reflex" is the gift of entry to a world wherein we are capable of transforming ourselves in order to learn from the horse.

The third concept on the path toward "letting go" is the "absence of past and future." It is one of the most difficult disciplines for us to enter into, possibly because it requires that we give up so much of what we consider uniquely human: anxiety, concern for appearance, dread, and insecurity. With our predilection for dwelling on the finiteness of history and anguishing over our hopes and dreams for the future, we rarely, if ever, "take life as it comes," moment by moment. But that is precisely what the horse needs us to do: live in the constant present. The more successful we are at abandoning the preconceptions and learned responses we are so fond of harboring, the closer we come to the "here and now" place wherein the horse resides. And, the more we are able to let go of our fears and apprehensions, the more possible it is to be with our horse, stride, by stride, by stride.

The "absence of past and future," above all, has to do not just with living in reality but with occupying a kind of upper-reality where all rogue thoughts and impulses glance off our "doing" at each moment. Impenetrable as we have become, we are left in focus with nothing but the horse and his "doing" at each moment. It is his world and we are acting in accordance with its principles, however alien they may feel to us a first.

But in fact, isn't reality often more amazing than what the mind alone can create? And more amazing still is the super-reality within the grasp of each moment.

In order for us to arrive at the optimum state of "letting go," there is one final concept that must be grappled with: the "non-judgmental mind." Since our proof of self often depends on the good or bad type of assessment, this is not an idea to which we come with ease. Nonetheless, the "non-judgmental mind" is prerequisite to the creation of free flowing, unstopped communication with the horse.

Perfection is not always announced with blaring trumpets and roaring crowds. In fact, what is correct is often much less than what we as riders expect it to be. Many times we do not allow our horses to be correct because we mistakenly want more, as if more, in this case, has anything whatever to do with forward, light, and round. The less we rely on proof and pass judgment, the more we are able to allow ourselves the luxury of the moment wherein the horse resides.

The absence of judgment frees us as riders. It enables us to be flexible and creative within each moment as it comes and to develop a "reflexive" gesture to whatever the horse gives us. Unencumbered by the rigidity of assessment, which takes us away from the moment-by-moment action of the horse, we are suddenly in the same place and time as the horse. How better to be as one, than to actually enter the manner and moment of perception as the horse? Surely the horse himself is not thinking, "there could have been a tad more bend in my shoulder-in" as he is traveling down the wall. How un-horse-like for him to be anything other than "with himself" at each moment. And how un-horse-like for him to critique that very essence. We would do well to emulate when seeking a closer union with him.

The process of "letting go" is forever, and within that great span of time, constant. There is nothing that can teach us how, nothing, that is, except the horse and our vigilant desire not to disturb his natural gifts but to partake of them graciously and with humility.

In the end, "letting go" is not something to get but something to be. It is an evolution of our inner selves with the horse as guide, and ultimately, a centering of each of us within ourselves and within the infinite vicissitudes of nature. It is our place: a place of serenity and quiet creativity.

Making the Connection

There is no doubt that it is far easier to train a horse than it is to teach a rider. The horse, after all, is quite equipped to do what he needs to do in order to function as a horse. His process of education does not culminate in changing him into something that he isn't. It might even be said that dressage changes the horse into something that he is already, only more so.

The person, however, is another story. He is not born to be a rider. He is intended to walk erect under his own impulsion. The person who wishes to ride dressage undergoes a far more complex and difficult alteration than the horse coming up through the levels. The rider has to reshape his body to both go along with, and later to influence the horse's movement. He must open his mind to new ways of evaluating the horse/human relationship. Most importantly though, he has to develop a new way of feeling through his mind and body that both receives from and sends to the horse. This is a multi-dimensional sensory language with the onus on the rider. It is his job to learn a vast repertoire of instant reflexes, both physical and mental, in answer to whatever the horse gives him; not an easy task and not one which every horseman would even want to explore.

But it is "feel" that gives dressage its compelling quality. At its best, it is a state where the purely physical is delivered with such ease that it becomes an effortless gesture of grace. Elusive though it is, it is the quality of "feel" that separates the great from the merely pedestrian horseman. It is the desire to tap into this sensation of the horse without disturbing him, that has produced the picture of selfless riding so prized by the "light" adherents. And, it is the sometimes unfathomable mystery of "connection" that enables the horse and rider to think and act as one.

Why is it that most riders achieve only the most rudimentary skills necessary to direct their horses while others rise to unimaginable levels of subtlety in their communication? The answer has first of all to do with outlook. Ask yourself. Are you a maneuverer or are you a negotiator? Do you want to unilaterally make the decisions or are you involved with the horse in coming to a decision? And even if you do make the decisions, are they the appropriate ones for what the horse gives you?

Most riders begin their education by cultivating the "maneuvering" aids. They learn signals or rote cues: go forward, stop, turn. And most riders spend the predominance of their riding time practicing and to a limited extent, refining these basics. Rarely, however is there much thought given to negotiation. There may be the whole gamut of postures present ranging from overt aggression to intense sympathy but the link is still missing: communication with the animal. We are telling but not waiting for a response. We are assuming but not listening. We have not allowed the two-way elasticity of partnership to happen.

Elasticity allows connection. Tolerance allows connection. And the desire to communicate also allows connection. When any point on a line is rigid or fixed for any more than an instant, there can be no connection. Connection relies on change, constant change, frequent, enlivened change. Hence, when any joint, ligament, or muscle in either the horse or rider is impaired in flexibility for whatever reason, this becomes a stopping point for the free flow of energy absorbing the movement of either. (This is also true for the rider's thought processes, incidentally.) Connection is a live language without stammers or stutters. It lives by flowing. This is why it is impossible to cultivate the soft back of a horse under a novice rider who is still struggling for his own balance. The same is true for teaching the rider to become soft and yielding on a horse who has learned to defend himself by hollowing his back. It is a reciprocal agreement: when one is tense and unyielding, the other is also. So how does the rider proceed in learning to become soft and allowing?

First it should be understood that it is the responsibility of the rider to undertake to train his body in flexibility and coordination before he expects it of his horse. The rider must be just as "through" as he wants his horse to be. His messages must travel from their genesis in his mind, through his body, all the way to their goal within the horse with no stopping along the way. They must be fluent and alive. As much as the horse will not present a "through" shape on his own, neither can the rider rely on his body to become astute to the needs of the horse without first being made aware of the impact his body has on the horse. To some degree, the horse knows and will show the rider how he wishes to be ridden if the rider is open and accepting and has learned to read and respond appropriately to the whole universe of sensations the horse offers.

So, knowing that it is desirable for both the horse and rider to become "through," and that "through" is connection, how is it possible to achieve this without sacrificing the integrity of either?

When contemplating the idea of connection, it will be found that there are actually three operations occurring simultaneously: connection within the horse, within the rider, and finally, between the horse and rider. Each is increasingly difficult to apprehend but attaining the first without changing the rider is impossible except through working exclusively from the ground. All three connections should be clear within the rider's mind before undertaking their development. This is not to say there won't be a great deal of backtracking and dovetailing between work on the rider and work essentially on the horse. There will be. This is, after all, the synchronization of two distinct entities both of whom have a particular sense of the way in which things should happen and a particular reaction when they do. Keep in mind though, that neither of you is totally correct in and of yourselves but that both of you need to arrive at certain compromises and softenings in order to allow connection to happen.

The Horse

Clearly, the easiest thing on this journey is first: teaching the horse to connect himself within his own being. Realization of his explosive instincts to fight or to run is the biggest hurdle. You are attempting to convince him that what he knows in every fiber of his being should not be his reality. His topline should not look like the bow of a ship with his eyes nervously scanning the countryside for mountain lions. Instead, he should rely on your fluent knowledge of his language and your consistent methods to replace his first choice of reaction to a new situation.

Whether this will happen or not depends on two things, both under the heading of trainer responsibility: a complete understanding of what is normal for the horse, and a thorough knowledge of the methods needed to change him including the flexibility to alter both understanding and methods when progress is stifled. In other words, you are the artist who comprehends both the natural medium with which you are working and the process by which, stroke by stroke, it becomes the final, cultivated work. You are combining nature and "man," hopefully without peril or lack of dignity for either. Your final product can only be enhanced by the quality of the détente you have created between these two unlikely partners.

This being said, it is time for the lunge line. Frequently, this is the first encounter a horse has with the "new order" of his universe and frequently it is not a regime he wishes to be a party to. Fortunately, the lunge can allow the horse the time and latitude he needs to become comfortable while placing a minimum of constraints on him. It is his time of discovery.

In the beginning you are simply asking the horse to go forward, stop at some convenient time in his mind, and to do this while attached to you via the lunge; not requests that are outside of the horse's understanding, incidentally. In addition, he will be doing this while learning to accommodate his body to the new demands of balancing on the circle. This is his first opportunity to study you so deliberate and consistent movement is a must. He will soon learn to read your body much as you are learning by studying his.

Mention should be made here that the methods used to "connect" the horse on the lunge are many and varied but that a method is only as valuable as the results it produces. Those that constrict the horse are not those that will truly connect him within his own body and teach him to carry himself. Lungeing should not be a process of inhibiting the horse's impulse to go forward in unity. It is a process of reshaping toward a position of strength, balance, and quietness of mind which in turn will happen only if the horse is allowed to move with some degree of freedom. It should appear to be his decision to go forward in lightness not excluding the notion of periodic playfulness should he be so inclined.

Bringing about the proper relation of freedom within influence is perhaps the most difficult quality of the horse/human relationship to achieve but it is central to any idea of harmony. Too much freedom and the horse will not understand how you want him to change. Too much influence and he will never learn to rely on what he has learned. Choice and adjustment of equipment, therefore, can make or break this relation.

Equipment which allows the horse to choose the correct position is best. Toward that end, running the lunge line through the snaffle ring and fixing it low on the girth for the beginning of each session gives some amount of freedom to the horse but also gives the trainer a degree of instantly adjustable influence. The trainer can both hold and give as necessity demands. He can also simply do nothing by allowing the horse to find his own way; a useful tactic if self-carriage is the desired goal. Most importantly though, the trainer has the means to bring the horse's head and neck down and to the inside by slight but frequent closings and openings of the line hand. The influence, therefore, becomes a matter of constant reminder rather than unyielding force.

The horse's reaction to this particular way of lungeing is always individual. Some resist by taking too much contact and race around with their heads up at the outer extremities of the line. Some exaggerate the curl of their necks to the inside. And still others go from one to the other, exploring their parameters. All horses, however, soon discover the "shape" that is comfortable for them and usually settle into a relaxed yet forward pace. This stage should be performed with as little influence from the trainer as possible. This is the horse's time to find out what he can about his movement. It is also a time for the trainer to assess the animal's nature and movement.

Once this has been satisfied, it is time for the outside side rein to be attached. First, this limitation places the horse in a position to give you his full attention without which, any attempt at communication would be futile. The horse must learn to watch, interpret, and trust your body movements. Second, it encloses his sphere of action to a more limited and less instinctively advantageous space. In other words, it makes it more difficult for the horse to resist what you are asking. And third, the single side rein adjusted long and low on the girth limits the lateral bend and connects the horse, rear to fore.

Here again, horses react in a number of ways to this new experience from backing away to protruding the underside of their necks. Keep the motion going. Relaxation will come as long as the horse is moving. It is central to connection that the hindquarters are active. The front is only shaped through the impulse of the energy from behind and through the unstopped, unconstrained, raised back. When there is no energy from behind, or when the flow of that energy does not go through the back, "on the bit" in front is only a pose. It is a headset, an artificial "look" pretending to be the real thing. It must be the whole horse we consider; not just the head.

Understanding that activity creates connection in the horse, the work in-hand can now be asked for. In the beginning you will ask for it intermittently on the lunge. It serves to further explain to the horse where his head and neck should be. Very early exercises will consist simply of taking hold of the inside ring of the snaffle and moving it in the horse's mouth, seeking that instant when he lets go and becomes soft. Immediately following this "light" moment, the horse should be sent back up to the trot on the lunge. When the giving takes place as soon as you take the snaffle ring in hand, move on to the work in-hand on a small circle. Move the head in toward you, out away from you and forward and down. When the neck remains stretched on top and the hardening of the mouth over the bit becomes only momentary, the horse is ready to begin sideways movement.

Again while still on the lunge, you will hold the inside snaffle ring, (side rein and lunge line for stronger horses), turn to the rear of the horse and with the whip, ask the horse to displace his haunches to the side. Most horses will instantly get hard in the mouth and go up with the head and neck. Stop, soften the horse in-hand, go forward on a circle and again, ask the horse to move his haunches away from you. Once this can be accomplished with a relaxed and stretched topline and with the rhythmic crossing of the hind legs, the horse is ready to begin the work in-hand off the lunge.

The beauty of the work in-hand is that it treats the whole of the horse in an intimate manner. The proximity of horse and human gives both a more profound knowledge of the other as it is not only the trainer who is the observer. The horse also gains an "eye" from this work. The rhythm of each body, the position of each in relation to the other, and the space as it surrounds and defines the movement becomes more tangible to both. It is a dancer's milieu.

Without question, work in-hand at the shoulder-in is work that will induce the horse to use his back. It both limbers the back laterally by the crossing of the hind legs and stretches it back to front by the down and forward advancement. A great lifting and rounding of the back can be observed by the trainer as the horse describes a small square at the walk,

Control of the extremities of the horse is often the focal point of the trainer without realizing that it is essentially the back of the horse that connects these extremities and allows the horse to use his entire body as a coordinated unit. "Riding the Back," or in this case, using the shoulder-in to soften and raise the back in the work in-hand produces many beneficial results within the horse not the least of which is the coordination of the two ends: the "on the bit" shape in front and the activity of the haunches behind. The horse becomes an arc with a slowly undulating connection in the middle of the arc. The horse is linked lengthwise through his back.

Too many backs are still. They become rigidly flat or defensively hollow, contracting or "leaving" the rider with nowhere to sit and the horse moving about in separate parts. This is primarily due to the misplaced focus of the trainer on one extremity or the other, usually the front. Once the head and neck are in a particular "frame," all else falls into place, right? This is not quite so. The truly "on the bit" horse creates energy from the haunches which moves through the softly undulating back to the shape and activity of the forequarters. It is through the back of the horse that the energy is "translated" to the front. It is here that the shaping takes place, not at the "face" of the horse.

This being understood, it can easily be seen that the shoulder-in is the exercise par excellence for the unlocking and the raising of the back. Though it is thought of as a collecting exercise, this can often be misinterpreted in practice leading to contortion and contraction rather than free flow and gentle shape. The shoulder-in is actually a "connecting" exercise, showing the horse how to use his incredibly unwieldy body without coming apart in two or three pieces. Done in the work in-hand, it gives the trainer the opportunity to actually see the process as it take place without having to concentrate on his own body while mounted.

It is one of the greatest pleasures of the work on-hand to not only feel what takes place but to be able to observe the change in the horse when he begins to work through his back. As if by some great realization or enlightenment on his part, the horse suddenly becomes beautiful. He moves as if he had for the first time, become aware of his entire body, as if this was what he had been born to do, as if he had been waiting all along for this moment of "connection."

The Rider

There is no way around it: the seat, the seat, the seat. It is mandatory for the person who wishes to ride well to have as his central goal the development of a correct and "intelligent" seat. This involves quite a bit more than simple learning to "go with the flow," adopting a hovering shape over the horse, or posturing in a rigid equitation position. Far from removing the rider from the movement of the horse's back, the effective dressage seat is one which lays within the movement, allowing the energy and vitality of the horse to flow through it. It is a seat which is both versatile and instantly adjustable to the necessities of the moment. And it is, as a matter of fact, the only way to make the horse comfortable in himself.

So how does one attain the unattainable? First, it should be stated that the way to learn the seat is not on a horse who does not carry himself well on the lunge. Any horse, simply because he's quiet, will not do. The horse who can teach is quite an advanced horse. He is able to move in an arc at all three gaits in a controlled and steady rhythm. He exhibits free range in the shoulders and hips, a raised back, and is comfortable maintaining the schooling as well as the working gaits. In short, he has been taught how to carry a rider in an efficient and unstressed manner. He displays such a picture of unity and comfort within himself in fact, that the rider is literally compelled to join him. It is an invitation that cannot be refused.

Most people come to the back of the horse in a state of fracture. Very little in their lives prepares them for the wholeness that is needed by the horse in order for him to perform, a wholeness and coordination not entirely physical. It is a totally complex and foreign world, albeit one with definite allurements.

The training of the body of the rider should begin on the lunge, at a square halt, with the repositioning of his body atop the horse. The alignment of the shoulders, hips, and heels should be accomplished by the instructor actually moving these areas softly and slowly until the correct line can be drawn. This will involve quite a great deal of further manipulation of the leg so that the rider understands the feeling of the long inner leg surrounding the horse. On no account should stirrups be used yet as this will tempt the rider to push away from the back of the horse and reinforce "learned" stiffness, particularly in the ankle and hip joints. At this point it should be underscored that the legs emanate from the hips which in turn must unlock and allow the seat (pelvis) to sink further into the back of the horse. It is from this that the rider gains security and indeed, his connection to the horse.

Connecting the rider within his own body depends on the discovery of his two seat bones and the ability to switch his focus from his extremities, (arms and legs), to his midsection. Use of the extremities are the temptations many riders resort to in moments of difficulty but they should never be the choices for those to whom classical riding is the goal. It is the seat that ties our bodies elastically together and allows our bodies to open and receive the movement of the horse.

Of what then does the seat consist? In totality, it is made up of the waist, lower abdomen, seat bones and crotch, the lower back, and the insides of the thighs. These are the parts of the body that when positioned correctly as to angle, surface, and tension, make it possible for the rider to sit in complete balance with the horse. These also provide the essential influences over the horse along with the use of weight which resides in and is controlled by these parts.

The seat then, is both an anchor and a compass. It gives the greatest amount of surface attachment via its wishbone shape and also predicts and navigates directional flow of the horse. By the subtle manipulation of the seat bones, the surrounding areas of the seat alter in shape and tension through each stride of the horse, always returning to the stasis point of relaxed attachment. It is the ability of the seat to stretch and breathe while maintaining contact that the horse finds both natural and acceptable. It represents the way things are in his own body and is understandable to him through this similarity.

The extent to which a rider is able to use his seat efficiently and with nuance is limited only by the gradations in feel he is able to recognize. It is largely a matter of heightened awareness. Sitting directly down with the shoulders balanced over the hips will give a feeling of width and lateral stability over the back of the horse. Riding on the back of the seat bones, (tucking the butt), gives a more pointed feel while tilting the seat bones slightly forward gives more of a rounded, cup feeling while easing the burden of weight on the horse's back. Each seat bone also has an inside and an outside which can be called into service depending on the adjustment or movement desired. The half pass left, for instance, emphasizes the inside of the left seat bone slightly in advance of the outside of the right seat bone. It is not so simple as a mere weight shift. It is a delicate distribution of angles within the rider's midsection that imparts the dictates yet the softness, of his message to the horse.

Called upon to choose which facet of the rider is the most important for the attainment of classical riding, it would have to be said that the three, body, mind, and spirit, are inextricably linked and cannot be separated. Each is an expression of the other. The body without the spirit is brutal. The mind without the body is futile. And the spirit without the other two is unrealized. Here again, it is the connection between these three aspects of the rider, each contributing to and modifying the other, that is the secret of the great horsemen.

It has been argued that the mind must understand first before the body can respond. It is also believed by some that the rote actions of the body produce thought in the mind. Either of these notions would be acceptable if they could be applied without exception to riding, but unfortunately, they cannot. The process of learning to ride well is far too complex and finely integrated within the person for it to be achieved through the dictates of one simple rule. Learning to ride is like learning to play a musical instrument. It requires the interaction between all human capacities in order for the work to be executed and when it is, to have any value other than that of mechanics per se. The producing of beautiful music, and by extension, the "dressing" of a beautiful horse, both rely on integration within the human being and how well he is able to create and keep a balance of the physical with the thoughtful under the guidance of the spiritual.

The mind of the rider is more than the governor of the body, yet less than the ability of the spirit to inspire and infuse with life. Its position lays somewhere in between the impulsive and the measurable, the artistic and the scientific.

One of the unique capacities of the rider's mind is that it allows us to sort and categorize sensations. It turns chaos into pattern and enables us to learn the intense and expressive language of the horse, as well as codify our responses. As a bonus, we are able to remember and reproduce those responses we wish to cultivate and refine for the benefit of mutual communication.

In this guise, the mind is acting remarkably like an additional sense, so quick is its impulse and direction. When operating in this manner, in fact, it is difficult to separate its reaction from that of the body's. This may be considered the least rational and deliberate capacity of the mind and the one most difficult to turn on. But it is the one which most closely acts as a true partner to the horse and is quick to answer whatever the horse presents. It is here where the rider takes on an air of transcendence with soft, non-directed eyes and a body which is all but motionless of its own accord. It is a special capacity of the mind for seeming to destroy its own assertiveness while actually operating at peak level.

Moving on to more measurable abilities of the mind, we find the inventive, problem-solving side to be most valuable not so much while working with the horse as when working away from the horse. This is the deliberate and logical urge of the mind to work through problems and to formalize whole constructs which it can test and ultimately prove. This capacity operates at a much slower rate and is the one easiest to call on for answers but it is not the one most easily comprehensible to the horse. Once it proves, it can be adamantly inflexible to his needs.

Along with problem-solving and a certain versatility in outlook, this facet of the mind has the ability to create images. This becomes important in the education of both horse and rider as a measure of change. Creating and recreating images of the most desirable goes far when trying to achieve them in reality. Picturing within the mind can be a constant reminder of the ideal without which, there can be no improvement.

And finally, a third ability of the mind may be called upon in the creation of the rider but more often than not, it is within this area that our downfall lurks: the critical mind. This involves the predilection we have for judgment, right or wrong, and most likely before we consider all the facts. The critical mind tends to block the rider from taking in what is around him and instead, gives out with commands, reprimands, and other manifestations of misguided certainty. It is the need for control that undermines our relations with horses and the judgmental mind which holds the reins.

Of course this capacity of the mind to judge can be turned to expose its more pleasing face; that of objectivity. Objectivity can best be considered the primary characteristic of the "open mind" once it has amassed considerable knowledge and realizes the vast amount yet to be attained. It is within the ability of the objective mind to be able to put things in perspective, compare where one is with where one wants to be, that can be of value when the "critic" wants to be in control.

Whether one wishes to accept it or not, most cultures of the world regard the human as comprised of three parts: body, mind, and spirit. We should do no less as riders if for no other reason than to fulfill a picture of ultimate balance and harmony with the horse, one of nature's own.

The spirit should be the center of good will toward the horse as reflected by the rider's attitude. It is an attitude of quiet acceptance and enjoyment of the horse as he is and constant wonder at the immense gift we have been given by his presence. There is no other inter-species "connection" that is quite as close in as many ways. It is a connection born of the spirit.

In no small way the horse uncovers what is within us. By virtue of his inimitable combination of qualities, we are placed in a position of extraordinarily delicate negotiations: too much and we destroy, too little and we are ignored. He shows us how to be in touch with him and with our inner selves. It should not escape us that he is nature's best ambassador and if given the opportunity, nature's most patient teacher.

Within this state of exchange which allows both mutual and self discovery, we are encouraged to change. As the horse teaches us to be comfortable with change, he demonstrates the futility of rigid, self-absorbed notions. We are suddenly sensitive to possibility, to actualization, and to the flow of impulses between two creatures. As he becomes the measure of our actions, motives, and even dreams, his affect will be profound. The more we open our perceptions, the more likely the revelation will come. If we are perceptive, the horse will change us in seemingly paradoxical ways, encouraging us to become both stronger and softer, more determined yet more humble. In short, he will help us to understand how, if not why, we fit into the natural world of which he is still so much a part. He will become our guide through the mystery of existence.

Horse and Rider

From the mundane to the ethereal, the union of human and horse represents the ultimate state of communication within diversity. This is an unusual connection and appears in its purest form, only within nature itself. Beyond the technical considerations, it is nature we are emulating when bringing the horse and rider together under the guidance of dressage.

As in any school or discipline, there exist vastly different interpretations on what that school should accomplish, not less so among the practitioners of contemporary dressage. Not only the means to the end but the end itself is open to individual preference. But there are certain qualities common to all good dressage, the difference being more a matter of degree and emphasis. Balance, suppleness, rhythm, and impulsion are the necessities of good dressage. "Connection" between horse and rider, that elusive unity of vision by design, is the necessity of dressage.

As stated earlier, neither the horse nor the rider can connect to each other without first attaining a certain amount of awareness and control within each of their bodies. This next phase, (as do the first two in the beginning stages), necessitates a third person orchestrating the steps along the way, directing the practice, and interpreting to the rider exactly what is happening under him. It goes without saying that this third person should be completely fluent in reading and to some extent controlling the horse from the ground.

The coming together of the horse and rider begins within the parameters of the lunge line. The introduction should take place only after the horse has been sufficiently schooled to maintain a position of roundness at all gaits including transitions. He should be able to lengthen and shorten on voice command, all the while keeping an uninterrupted rhythm. And, very important for teaching the rider, the horse should be confirmed in the school trot, a trot frequently preferred by the old masters over that of the working trot. This is a slow, cultivated trot that does not place extreme demands on the body of the rider. The school gaits are nonetheless forward and should give the rider the correct feel of movement while inspiring confidence by their less demanding tempo.

Beginning in the rounded (not hollow) halt, time should be given to positioning the rider flexibly on the horse. Manipulation of each leg from the hip joint must be done gently at first but enough so that when back in position, the rider will begin to sink with his seat bones into the raised back of the horse. This will become a reference point for the rider and should always be returned to when the connection between the back of the horse and the rider's seat bones is lost. The rider should also be asked to focus on and memorize these particular touching points as they will become the anchors once alignment of the body is understood.

While maintaining this contact, the upper leg should also be gently manipulated so that the inner thigh drapes lightly around the horse with the knee joints turned inwards. It should be stressed that it is not the back of the leg that makes contact but the longer and less muscular inner leg. This involves the rotation of the joints inward, (the opposite of the opening of the joints outward as in ballet), and until this position can be maintained comfortably and without stress, the temptation will be for the rider to grip with and shorten the legs. This, as many have found, proves useless when aiding the horse as the leg is pulled away from his sensitive sides.

As de la Guérinière states, "the legs must breathe" with the horse and cannot if they are nowhere near him. This elastic and even "organic" contact must become reflex in the rider if he is to aid the horse in the higher level movements by lifting (massaging) the horse with his legs. The sensation of the breathing horse is also inextricably linked to the rider's feel for the horse's rhythm. Without it, many incorrect judgments can be made as to speed and impulsion, interrupting the natural flow of the horse. The "breathing legs" are not just a fanciful description; they are an integral part of connection to the horse.

While still seated at the halt, the entire picture should be considered both from the side and from the rear. Are the rider's shoulders balanced over his hips? Is there a slight arc to the back? Do the arms hang straight from the shoulders with elbows at the sides? As seen from the rear, are the rider's shoulders at even height? Is the waist level side to side? Do both legs reach evenly down the sides of the horse? If these conditions are met, the rider is ready to move into the walk.

Inasmuch as the rider may get the wrong impression at the halt, namely, that his body is to rigidly adhere to the "form" just created, it is important that frequent transitions are performed between the walk and halt. This is a difficult time for the rider. Having just mastered the correct positioning of his body at the halt, he is now quite aware of just how easily things fall apart when the horse moves. It is at this juncture that explanations of "supple yet shaped" should be entered into.

When the horse moves, the rider should allow the movement to affect his body to the extent that he does not prevent the movement from expressing its full extent. In other words, he must go along with and absorb the movement, transforming it through his seat and back so that the rest of his body remains relatively still. It is the midsection of the rider's body that negotiates what the horse gives, not the extremities. By removing the need for hands and legs in the beginning, the rider learns not to rely on them to control the horse or to maintain his own precarious balance. And, by extension, when they do come into play, he is more apt to employ them as the subtle aids that they are meant to be.

Certain other, more useful skills can be introduced at this time, ones that will form an intimate connection with the horse once they are revealed and understood by the rider. These are less ostensible but utterly meaningful to the sensitive animal we hope to cultivate.

If we look at the horse as a dancer would, we soon discover that he has dimension, that he occupies space, and that he carves out of that space an infinite variety of ever-changing shapes. It is this constant flow of shape that we wish to comprehend when seeking connection with the horse.

As soon as the rider is made aware of the movement of the horse through his seat and back, he should be shown how to influence the horse with the subtle shadings of position and weight. This is dependent not only on the relaxation of the rider's midsection but also on this awareness of an internal and centered "integrity" apart from outside influence. This "soundness" has its roots in the rider discovering a soft position of "going along" which also has the crucial characteristic of being the position from which the rider may influence the horse. It is the same position for both, simply with different emphases. So, to not interfere with the horse's movement and to purposely interfere, both require essentially the same functional shape of the rider's body with only slight and momentary modifications.

Now is the time for the rider to begin, without hands or legs, to discover just what impact his body can have on the horse. This is usually an epiphany for most and a discovery that greatly benefits later riding. Rather than relying on the all too tempting hands to slow or stop or the legs to push and grip, the student learns a closer connection with his mount based on his seat, back, and torso.

While still on the lunge, the rider is asked to consider his body in relation to the horse's. Does each seat bone connect with a hind leg as the horse walks on? Can the rider both allow his seat to be lifted and then interrupt the flow of the walk deliberately by exerting his seat ahead of the rhythm? Has the student been made aware of "following" the horse's back? In other words, does the rider understand that when the weight is greater on one seat bone, the horse will naturally follow underneath to maintain his own balance?

Whether projecting direction to the horse by looking, by turning the shoulders, or by shifting the weight, it is all part of the integrated body needed for dressage. Each section of the rider's body must contribute to the same message if the horse is expected to understand. If the rider looks to the right, his right shoulder must move back and his right seat bone must sink slightly. Any less, and the rider is out of tune with himself and therefore, out of tune with the horse. Even if the horse is thoroughly schooled, he still cannot be expected to comprehend mixed messages or those which are garbled due to a lack of "throughness" in the rider.

Once the student has mastered the understanding of connection as it pertains to his responsibility apart from hands and legs, he is ready to take on the task of adding these potentially disruptive influences. From the security achieved through the relaxed yet adhesive seat, the legs can now be added. Particular attention should be given to the knee and ankle joints, especially when stirrups are added. They are frequently overused and tend to place the leg too far forward, opening to the outside. The thigh and lower leg should not change with the ball of the foot merely dusting the stirrups. For this, the leg has to stay in position even though the tendency is for the leg to suddenly hike itself within a shorter, cramped position. The thigh must remain long, balancing the top heavy human torso.

By the time the rider has come this far, the addition of hands and reins should not pose too great a challenge. From the work in-hand, the student should have gained an appreciation for just how delicate the rein influence can be. With his new focus on "body" riding he will have gained the confidence to keep his hands where they belong in the hierarchy of aids: only as the final shaping tool. Even in the deliverance of aids, it is the rider's body that sends the message first. It is the rider's hands that modify and make clear that message secondarily. This is the necessary order: seat and legs first, hands last. Working both together only produces tension in the horse since he needs time and space to react to any message. Then and only then will the horse be able to flow from one stride to the next, from one movement to the next.

Many words have been spoken and written on using the hands but rarely is this explained to the rider. (The same, incidentally, is true for using the legs.) Simply put, use of the hands means a momentary closing of the fingers of one or the other hand, followed immediately by a release. Whether you are softening on the inside rein or positioning the horse more fully into the outside rein, the sequence is the same, varying only in intensity and duration. Like the legs, the fingers too move in a kind of breathing or massaging fashion, always returning to a position of resilience. In the case of the hands, the rider is constantly testing the horse for self-carriage; the closing shapes, the opening allows. Nothing is ever static with the reins. Even in the ideal halt, there are little pulsations running through the reins asking again and again to stay, balance, and maintain. A more decided and momentary opening of the fingers sends the horse forward.

Once the rider understands that the hands in and of themselves possess a certain degree of weight when in closed contact on the reins, it is time for him to learn to give away that weight by carrying it himself. It is by constantly varying that weight toward the lightest end of the spectrum that the horse learns to rely on himself for balance and carriage. It is also the prime indication of the independent seat and hands so sought after. When the rider does not use his hands for what is lacking in his seat and legs, he is ready for subtle negotiation.

At this point it will be useful for the student to experiment with alternate ways of distributing the reins between the fingers. As the rein is moved up a slot so that it is carried between the third and fourth fingers, the hand becomes detectably lighter to the horse. And when it is moved up again with just the thumb and forefinger in contact, it is the lightest. It is not enough, however, for the fingers to be light; they must also connect with the horse. In other words, they must receive accurately, assess, and transmit back approval or modification. This occurs in fractions of seconds and must develop within the rider so that it becomes akin to reflex. There is no time for deliberation here. Communication with the horse necessitates acute perceptions and the rapid responses present in dialogue.

For both horse and rider, frequent return to the basics during the schooling session will keep the work progressive. For the horse, this may mean back to work in-hand to reestablish that resilient lightness that was lost when the rider become too firm and unyielding with the reins. For the rider, it may mean back to positioning again at the halt with no stirrups. When position, lightness, good will, and concentration are lost in either, it is better to go back, establish calmness, and then proceed. Nothing can be gained by prolonging a fault. The nature of connection demands not overlooking what happens between horse and rider, but opening up, improving, and refining the quality of the meeting. Any less, and the promise of true partnership remains unfulfilled.

Conclusion

Connection is the substance of dressage. It is the vast common ground of a newly created world where horse and rider discover how they fit together. This has less to do with the mechanics of riding the horse well or conditioning him to carry than it has to do with those "touching" points of personal nature: conviction, attitude, compassion, and the ultimate surrender of self that each undergoes in order to mutually praise, comfort, and be with the other. Neither by himself can have such knowledge. Neither by himself can rise as high.

> The way is deep,
> not different.
> Stay there.

The Way to Dressage

Table of Contents

	Preface	79
Chapter 1	What is Dressage?	80
Chapter 2	The Lure of Illusion	82
Chapter 3	Transitions	85
Chapter 4	The Whip	90
Chapter 5	The Rider's Position	93
Chapter 6	A Picture of Energy	99
Chapter 7	The Two-by-Four Lesson	102
Chapter 8	Go Left, Go Right	106
Chapter 9	The Snake on the Rock	114
Chapter 10	Training vs. Conditioning	116
Chapter 11	Starting Shaman	120
Chapter 12	The Mentor	140

Preface

Little words generate immense ideas – and so it is when choosing a title.

Ideally, the title should not give too much, which could be clumsy or appear defensive, nor too little, which might not inform enough or even become misleading. That is the dilemma. And that is the reason for the rather subtle change in titles introducing the three sections of this volume.

In the first section, "The Way of Dressage," the word "of" implies that what is about to follow is already in place and that what is offered is abstracted from it. It is solid, certain, full of assuredness.

In this section, "The Way to Dressage," the word "to" does just the opposite. It suggests a path that is to be taken but also implies a step back, a reevaluating. The journey is being taken but is neither complete nor certain.

And so we have an apt parallel going on between life and dressage: from youth, section 1, through maturation, section 2 to…

We will just have to wait until we're there.

—Susan Medenica

What is Dressage?

Explaining "dressage" is a little like trying to explain "life." By the time you come up with a definition, you see the need to change it. And of course, while you are changing it, something else escapes and you see the futility of your endeavor, for both "life" and "dressage" derive their meanings from an ongoing evolution and as such, are never complete or finite.

We can, however, describe that evolution without impeding it if we can follow a line of thought that is less material, more conceptual. And so we will begin our definition of "dressage."

Simply put, dressage is training. This is the first principle and the underlying foundation. When we think of training, however, we tend to think of patterns, school figures, and the horse executing such and such a movement; the haunches-in, for example. But unfortunately, this is not training, it is conditioning and the two are quite different. The classical training of the dressage horse focuses on constant improvement in the horse's "natural" gaits: the walk, trot, and canter. This is progressively achieved by amplifying them in terms of strength, suppleness, brilliance, and by extension, self-expression. From this perspective, the figures and exercises are but a means to a goal, not a goal in themselves. The figures are the servants of the gaits.

By contrast, conditioning, which permeates most horse-related disciplines, involves the mechanical reward and punishment for a given behavior, having little to do with the way in which it is performed. Thus, the conditioning perspective would hold that the shoulder-in at the trot is the achievement. From the training perspective, however, it is the increased engagement of the hind legs in the trot, (resulting from the practice of the shoulder-in), that is the goal. It is always the enhancement of the horse that is the prime motivation in training, not the "trick."

The second principle in the education of the dressage horse is that the horse must be made available to the trainer. This means that the horse is ultimately open and responsive to the merest hint or suggestion, culminating in effortless movement that is prompted simply by thought. (This of course, does not occur apart from the creation of the gaits but within that creation.) The effective trainer is always receptive but directive as well, based on his knowledge of how the horse communicates with other horses and how he himself can communicate in like manner without actually being a horse himself.

Two-way communication is essential and for it to occur, a mutually understandable language must be in place and operative. Based on what is "natural" for the horse, (what he would likely do without our intervention), this language is one of extreme subtlety and nuance, developed and refined through his interaction with the herd. What he says to another horse, he will say to us if we understand that language and are open to it. This, of course, is easier said than done since we often erroneously assume that other creatures have no language because they do not speak ours. The ultimately peaceful order in which horses reside, however, should leave no doubt that language is in full operation here. Would that the human race could communicate so well!

In its first two incarnations, dressage assumes the mantles of movement and communication. In movement, the horse has become round, rhythmic, and relaxed. In communication, he has become soft and receptive, acquiescing to the merest hint of a request. And so through training, the horse has risen to the level where he can begin to communicate through this movement. He has gone from the purely physical where he moves through space at the trainer's direction, and is beginning to select, (through the trainer's allowance), those times when his own notion of movement is desirable and appreciated. He has begun to push the boundaries (and so have we in our definition of dressage!)

But it is the ability to work within boundary and still come up with something new and personal that is so compelling in dressage. What good is a system if it does not allow? What good are rules if they cannot be risen above? And, how can we have definition if we are not all-inclusive?

The answers to these questions are given life in our third and final incarnation: when dressage becomes dance. First, the partnered dance with the trainer participating, then the solo dance in self-carriage where the horse evolves into the best of himself and the trainer merely admires. And the evolution will continue when foundation leads to fancy, restraint advocates liberation, and the discipline of dressage engenders the play of dance. Neither life nor dressage can remain the same; they both must evolve to have substance. In a way, they cannot help but change. In another way, they cannot help but dance.

The Lure of Illusion

Nowhere is illusion more prevalent than when humans deal with horses. It seems we have a difficult time accepting and interacting with the horse's reality and prefer instead to place ourselves into a visually satisfying, Pollyanna kind of world. In this world there are no broken fences, no flies, our horse wins every class, is worth far more than we paid for him, and never, ever, causes us to be afraid. This fabrication, of course, is a feeble attempt to be in control of that which we will never control. It is also proof that we secretly think of ourselves as preeminent over all that is apart from us. Thus, it becomes the ultimate disrespect for creation even though that creation inhabits the reality we must face. And such is the nature of illusion.

Illusion is a kind of fiction. In this made-up story, the deception arises when only the self is considered, the "little me" that is nothing but appetite. And the self is nourished and rewarded when all has a place, is in place, and doesn't move from that place. It is like adjusting the rider's body on the halted horse. All is well – until the horse moves. Then the rider comes undone. Illusion is, that all is well. It glosses over what is really there and puts forth a pleasing picture instead. But, it is a lie, albeit an alluring one.

Poor, scared creatures that we are, we all seek something finite, something known, something tangible to help us along. When we don't have any of these, we, like the rider on the horse who moves, come undone too. This is why we fabricate instead of experience. It is far easier to live in a lie than it is to live in reality for reality is uncomfortable and often presents a picture other than what we wish others to see.

The world of illusion has everything to do with our feelings of comfort and security and our desire to feel good about ourselves as we worry about what others think of us. In and of themselves, these are not totally bad preoccupations but what they lead to is nothing short of disastrous; to ourselves, our horses, and by extension, the world and all in it. This overwhelming concern for self leads to a kind of hierarchal view where thought is stifled and regimentation is employed to keep everything in place. We are allowed to go up, (the envy of others), go down, (the object of pity), but never above or below. These latitudes are not permitted since there is no way to measure them. They, for their part, soar and delve into the realm of reality which most do not wish to recognize, let alone enter. But this is precisely the land of the horse and the area in which we can meet him face to face without illusion about who he is or who we are in his presence.

Describing reality in terms of above or below simply puts reality always at odds with surface, always something else, something other than. This in turn denies the power of the eye and rightly so, since the eye deceives. And when the eye deceives, something else happens: the mind is fooled. The mind has no way of knowing it has been duped and continues to register these surface messages offered by the eye and will continue in this fashion until a radical change is made and that radical change is this: that without sharp eyes, there is surprising depth and that when you stop looking, you start seeing. In other words, material has become substance. Appearance is attractive but it is not where the horse is. The raised head and neck of the horse means something further to another horse. It may mean "Stay away." It may mean "Welcome." Its significance is not in its expression but in its substantial meaning to the other horse. And this is where humans fail. We wish to see the pleasing picture, the glossy surface of our world but this has dire consequences when applied to our relations with the horse. We end up ignoring his intent, as if he never had any at all. We deprive him of significance.

Aside from the pure ignorance and silliness of humans, (two of our more endearing qualities when compassionately viewed), there is yet another human trait that frequently arises when the human is disappointed: projection. Living in illusion necessarily leads to dissatisfaction and this dissatisfaction most often targets the horse, is projected onto the horse, and erroneously assumes that the horse is at fault. The logic here is skewed. The horse is simply a horse. He has no ulterior motive; but we may. It is part of illusion to project onto others our inadequacies so that we appear wise or in control or beautiful, handsome, smart, or rich; all the false, multicolored trinkets of our make-up. But the horse has no way of adjusting to or knowing this. He cannot tell you, "Hey. I can't possibly balance both of us around a corner when your inside shoulder is in front of your outside. Practice being in alignment with me. Help me to do what you think you are asking of me." And this is the job of the enlightened instructor: to translate to the student who the horse is, and to keep him mindful that it is his job to learn, change, and assist the horse. There is no other way.

In the world of illusion then, we take up residence either in over-control or excuse. Because we tend to think a great deal of ourselves, (probably a survival mechanism), we erroneously consider the horse our rightful extension and make decisions and judgments about him which subject him to the artificiality of our own views. He cannot live here. The fact that he is not in this world in the first place never occurs to us. We should be giving the horse what is acceptable and understandable to him; not what we think is good for him. This requires that we learn his vocabulary and that we are able to use it in concepts that he first pays attention to and second, responds to; no easy task for the human with his predilection for busy-ness and judgment.

And here we should make no mistake. The horse's natural state has little to do with the state in which humans find comfort. In both management and training, we would do well to become scrupulously honest about who the horse is before we attempt to bring him into our fabrication of who he is. His natural world is mud, snow, dust, rain, and bugs. His training world is pushing or pulling against pressure, fleeing from sudden sound or movement, contracting his body against restriction, and putting forth as little energy as possible when asked to go forward. This is who he is and we must understand and enter into his "what is" before we can ever hope to become partners with him. But first, it is we who must change. In short, we must first become who the horse needs.

Training the horse then is far more about training ourselves to have no illusions. It is about the process of humbly becoming. And what is it that we become? Fellow residents in reality.

Transitions

A transition is simply a change. If we take it apart and examine its general structure, we find that it consists of three distinct parts: where we are at the time, where we will be, and the passage between the two. The before and after do not pose difficulties but the passage does. Like leading a horse from the stall to the paddock, he is comfortable while in the stall and while in the paddock. It is the passage between the two where his emotional level is apt to rise. And such is the nature of change.

Horses are, after all, perfect people. They hate change. Both will do all in their power to avoid it, first, because it requires effort, and second, because it places them face to face with the unknown. Both work and uncertainty are uncomfortable prospects at best and require from both horse and rider a kind of flexible balance; an evolving balance, if you will. This evolving balance takes place in each successive moment.

Transitions are the rehearsals of change. To say that they are movements in and of themselves is not entirely unjustified. If we could practice nothing but transitions, we would be well on our way to mastery over ourselves and our horses. Good transitions consist of solid preparation and predictable outcome, but without perfecting that instant of passage, there cannot be continuity or flow.

What else is movement but inevitable transition? From one stride to the next, from one leg leaving the ground and returning to it, all is change in the service of movement. What is particular to dressage, and indeed all the time arts such as music and dance, is that unlike the graphic arts of painting and sculpture, nothing is captured and unchanging. The very substance of dressage is movement; the very nature of movement is change. In the case of the horse, stasis, or stability in movement equals balance and so we have an entirely different concept to work with: the core of sameness that carries constant change into a balanced shape through space and time. In other words, we are grappling with the idea of what it is that does not change within change.

This is a difficult concept for us as riders in particular since we tend to think in terms of outcome, not process. The goal-oriented rider is missing the point, however, since "the point" is ever-changing, the destination a convenient construct but a bitter disappointment. To have a goal puts us ahead of the horse but as soon as the goal is arrived at, puts us behind the horse. It is illusion at its most treacherous for in flow, it is always something else. In most cases, the very act of thinking what it is puts us either behind or ahead of the movement. We have come from nowhere; we are going nowhere. This is the ongoing stability of movement.

And so, transitions make us confront the uncomfortable notion of change. The conventional transitions in dressage, those between and within the gaits, are by no means the only times in which the horse and rider move from one place of stability to another.

There are four other and even more crucial transitions to understand for what they are: shifts in anatomical function and therefore, expression. These are basic to what we ask of the horse in terms of his balance and acquiescence to moving through space. They are important when starting the young horse as they introduce some degree of discomfort to his view of life and resulting customary behavior.

Since transitions are all about practicing change, the first "basic" transition the horse is confronted with and indeed, the one that follows him all the way into and through his training, is the change from inertia to movement. Anyone who has ever started a young horse can attest to the fact that moving him forward can initially be quite a challenge. And anyone who has ever collected the horse in place for the halt to canter transition knows the difficulty of this concept. This transition, in and of itself, encompasses all that we ever ask of the horse: to stop, to go. Everything is a combination of the two. At the halt there is the energy of potential. In movement, there is the energy of realization. What else is piaffe but the quintessential example of stop and go in close succession?

If the horse has been prepared thoroughly from the ground with work on the lunge and a heavy dose of work in-hand, the initial mounting should be an anticlimax. In most instances, the horse will find it more difficult to understand movement while mounted than he will the halt. It is a question of balance. Even in the halt, however, the young horse will display little shifts of weight to accommodate his new obligation. This, of course, becomes more acute when forward movement is added with the transition between the two full of lumps and bumps at first. By the time the horse is fully "dressed," however, the halt changes from inertia to potential by virtue of the containment of energy which is ever ready to be expressed in whatever movement is desired. Inertia to movement is a dynamic transition, probably the most dynamic the horse ever makes whether it is at the end or in the beginning of his training.

The second transition to be considered is that of changing direction and thereby changing emphasis within the horse's body. Each horse finds it more difficult to move certain parts of his body one way or the other and changing direction emphasizes this inequality. Common signs of difficulty, usually more so when changing from left to right, are normal for the horse and usually manifest themselves in a number of predictable ways: the head and neck rise, the tempo slows or speeds up, the horse continues the new direction in counter-flexion, and the new inside hind leg moves to the outside rather than underneath the horse's body.

At this point it is absolutely essential that the rider understand the mechanics of the horse's movement from both sight when watching, as in the work in-hand, and blind when mounted. What is normal and what is correct are two different things and the rider must instantly assess which is which. Passing the horse from right to left or left to right requires both freedom and boundary; freedom to swing and boundary to carry. The rider must both see and feel when there is a restriction or an escape in the horse's body and instantly allow or curtail a shoulder, a hip, a nose, even at times, an eye.

When it is the goal for the horse to be both forward and round, a third transition becomes an absolute essential both for suppling and strengthening and for reminding the horse to stay soft in the contact. This is the transition from straight to bend and back again from bend to straight.

It is best to introduce this concept into the training right from the beginning work in-hand even before mounting. Not only does it make the horse more malleable in his body, but he becomes almost instantly more accepting in his mind of the rider's requests.

So for the horse, what does this actually involve? Fundamentally, the horse will use strength or speed when confronted. By changing frequently from bend to straight the rider is playing with the horse's instincts, but using them to his own advantage. When the horse bends his body, his forward thrust, hind leg directly to foreleg in a straight line, is offset thereby diminishing his power. In other words, he softens. This is often a good thing for the rider since the temptation to use the hands as a way to curtail forward movement is usually dominant. Any way in which this predilection can be diverted is wise and starts the rider on the path of correct thinking right from the start: the hands are always an afterthought.

The transition from straight to bend is additionally an excellent way to introduce the horse to the idea that the leg or the whip or the cluck do not only mean "go forward." Far too often this is the programmed way in which the horse responds as in the "open show" method of schooling. But conditioning to a cue is not yet training. Training requires that the horse rise to understand levels of meaning and shades of variation which indicate the way in which he should proceed, not just that he should proceed. By alternating between bend and straight we are introducing this concept to the horse and refining his receptive vocabulary. Additionally, his attention to us is increased since we are varying our requests often and requiring the horse to think, not just respond.

In the initial use of this transition, the perfection of any given bend will not be achieved either in the work in-hand or the mounted work. What is gained, however, is that the horse learns to isolate individual body parts and focus his attention on detail. In other words, his neuro-pathways become activated simply by asking his right hind leg, for instance, to step in front of the left hind, or cross the left hind, or follow directly behind the right fore; the parameters of bend to straight.

There is an old saying from the annals of dressage that in order to straighten the horse, we must first bend the horse. Puzzling at first, it becomes clearer when we attempt to straighten a naturally crooked horse who does not allow the aids to penetrate his body. We may get an initial reaction from the horse but in no way can his response be limited or expanded. In the shoulder-in, for instance, the first problem is getting the horse to move away from pressure, i.e., to shift his rib cage to the outside. The second and more knotty problem, however, is to get the horse to understand that he is also to be held in place by the pressure of the outside leg of the rider. Only when these two opposite leg requests are in place is it possible to bend or straighten the horse. The leg means go away; the leg means stay. And between these legs is the horse allowing himself to be bent or straightened.

The final transition of importance in the basic schooling of the horse is that of purposely changing tempo. This is a "first you create it, then you recreate it" situation for it is only by upsetting the stasis in the horse's mind that he will ever be truly on the aids. In other words, the horse must learn what we mean by "rhythm," or the consistently equal time between footfalls, but then allow himself to be changed to one of the myriad gradations of faster or slower footfalls. For the horse to be locked into a tempo means he is not available to the aids of alteration. He may very well make the changes between gaits with predictable results, but the changes within gaits will be impossible. He will have one walk, one trot, and one canter, and will change gaits rather than change tempo.

It is important at first, therefore, to establish tempo, (which incidentally will produce a consistent rhythm), and once the horse is able to maintain it, change it to a faster or slower tempo and establish rhythm again within the new tempo. This is another way of assuring that the horse is being trained, not just conditioned. The conditioned horse acts out of routine, is adamant about what he knows, and is difficult to change. The trained horse, to the contrary, waits for the rider to ask and is willing to try new "variations on a theme" when asked. In other words, he is totally available, mind and body, to the rider and will change as often and as much as the rider requests. Programming, per se, has no place here since it is change that keeps the horse's mind open and even to a degree, creative. Inasmuch as movement is the expression of the horse, it is perhaps not too farfetched to say that the horse has the capacity of creativity, if and only if he has not been stifled by repetitive, rote work, just for the sake of work.

At the onset of schooling, it will be observed that in terms of gaits, the horse will offer what is comfortable for him. This is understandable since by himself he is a model of energy efficiency. But alas, what is comfortable for him is not necessarily what is best for him once the rider is added. Right from the start then, the horse should learn to give more than what he offers; a transition in itself and one that should become endemic to his personality. This is no less than the display of perfect trust in the human surpassing the horse's reliance on his own instinct; a true sacrifice from the horse's perspective.

In terms of changing tempo, we are directly confronting the horse's comfort zone and asking him to move out of it again and again and to increase or decrease effort as requested. In this sense, what he chooses is never what we are satisfied with. Our response to what he gives us is always, "no, not that, but this." In this way we are doing no less than deliberately practicing change and engaging in a personal conversation that is without end.

Movement is exciting to the horse and by changing tempi, we are also raising or lowering his emotional level. This in turn affects how he carries his body as he moves along a spectrum ranging from complete relaxation to intense alertness. Different speeds will physically affect the quality of contact, the shape of the top line, elevation of the legs, facility of movement, articulation of the joints and hence, suspension or the lack thereof. This outlines the dilemma of the play between movement forward and movement upward. Far too often at the lower levels, the horse is compelled to rush forward at a tempo that may induce the "tracking up" of the working gaits, but allows for no "air" time or suspension. The horse takes on a flat appearance and often "brings up dust" with his toes rather than clearly articulating the upward rotation of his joints. It is only by playing between the thrust of more speed and the lift of less speed that the horse can advance further into collection and by extension, self- carriage.

Transitions are difficult for the horse because they undermine his security. Staying is more comfortable for him. Why should he go through that intervening moment of uncertainty where physical, mental, and emotional balances are challenged?

Precisely because the horse has an innate resistance to doing what he has not done before, change makes him flexible, comfortable, and available to his rider. What the horse is programmed to do, he does well, but when confronted with anything out of his "frame of reference," he will resist or possibly refuse. It is only by expanding his frame of reference, in other words, his customary behavior in and of itself, that we can ease his insecurities and tap into his intelligent nature. Transitions serve us well when seeking this level of communication for it is precisely the transition that removes the horse from instinct and elevates him to a true thinking partner.

The Whip

The whip is an instrument of great capacity, limited only by the mind and skill of the employer. Whether it creates the desired response from the horse is, like any other aid delivered, entirely the responsibility of the trainer. The language is there; the trainer must become a fluent speaker, however.

All animals read the whip. They do not need to be taught and no translation is necessary. The horse in particular, keenly aware of the melding of time and space, speed and proximity, is receptive to this language precisely because the whip contains the impulse for both movement and stillness and all gradations in between. In a sense, it is alive with those messages which are too subtle for words or heels and thus it becomes the conveyor of intimacy between horse and trainer. To use it correctly opens up a limitless vocabulary. To use it otherwise would be to diminish its magic.

Within purely technical parameters, the whip expresses intent through speed, duration, sound, position, and intensity. This is the way the horse perceives it and the greater our mastery over these capacities, the more precise our message. In other words, the whip is the direct descendant of our thought and as such, will in and of itself express confusion or clarity to the horse depending on what is in the mind of the trainer.

The velocity at which the whip moves through air has a direct and immediate influence on the horse. The quicker the whip, the quicker the response from the horse and conversely, the slower the movement of the whip, the slower the response. For animating the horse, the whip will succeed where the legs of the rider, which tend to suppress movement, will fail. The rapidity of the whip contains the element of surprise which always provokes the startle response from the horse. We then have something to work with and can direct the horse into an appropriate shape. Once the horse has been "awakened" to its existence, the mere presence of the whip will elicit forward movement for a while. Periodically, (not routinely!), it will have to reawaken as the prompt response from the horse diminishes. The whip is always used in answer to what the horse gives, always as a consequence of his activity or his inertia.

In connection with speed is duration; both how long the whip is in the air and how long it is in contact with the horse. The longer it is in contact with the horse, the less its impact. Like the constant leg, the horse soon learns to ignore anything too long-lived without change, (a good caveat for the way in which we live our lives, by the way)! The same applies to not touching the horse. He will soon become dull to its presence because he has never experienced it except as a threat. The follow-through has been missing. The whip must come alive at apt times when its particular message is warranted.

If the horse has been dulled by too frequent feel of the whip, the sound of it will surely make him alert. The crack of the lunge whip or the rapid back and forth whoosh of the riding whip slicing through the air will often succeed where the touch will not. The hearing of the horse is keen and addressing that sense can be a more effective means of reaching him. It is as if the horse recognizes that you have the knowledge of who he is under the surface and the sound meets him there directly. The wise trainer always addresses the personal in the horse, not merely the outward manifestation.

The position in which the whip resides at any given moment tells yet another story. Like the horse, the whip has a back end, (go forward, go away from), and a front end, (stop or yield). The horse is very aware of the "conformation" of the whip and depending on which end is presented to him, will offer a different response. For instance, when the trainer stands facing the horse and slightly ahead of the shoulders on the left side, with the whip in the right hand, reins in the left, the proximity of the whip to either end of the horse will give a different message. If the lash end of the whip is moved nearer to the haunches, the horse will either move forward, (if he is on a wall), or move his haunches to the right, away from the whip if there is nothing to block him. If, on the other hand, the butt end of the whip is moved toward him and in front of his nose, he will stop altogether or move his head away. The butt end of the whip can "close the door" to forward movement or initiate sideways movement of the shoulders; the lash end of the whip can either move the haunches forward or sideways, depending on where it is in relation to the horse and more importantly, how it is directed by the quick comment from the reins.

Inasmuch as the horse is capable of perceiving the most miniscule movement in his environment, the position of the whip in relation to him does not go unnoticed. Therefore, the neutral position is fundamental to his understanding of intent. This is the "you're fine; maintain what you are doing" message. In general, the whip is away from his body and held with fingers slightly ajar. Stillness is of the greatest importance here as any inadvertent movement of the whip will necessarily undermine the precision of the message. The sooner the trainer learns to think with the whip, the better. The horse is ever perceptive.

An examination of the whip would not be complete without the mention of intensity. This is the most common association in people's minds and usually leads to thoughts of harshness. This, of course, is entirely erroneous if the whip is in the hand of the studious and practiced trainer.

The intensity with which the whip is used is nothing less than the drama of the whip for it has the power in and of itself to attract and keep the attention of the horse. And, it possesses this power because it is a direct expression of the mind of the wielder, for better or worse. From the thought to the touch, (the intent to the expression), its impact can range from a caress to a stinging reprimand on opposite ends, and include all shades of meaning in between. As such, a vast vocabulary is available complete with precise accent and nuance.

And one final thought: the whip is like the language of poetry where the word and the thought are inseparable. Whatever the whip does, it does so as a visible extension of the trainer; at least that is how the horse perceives it. The movement of it is not seen as accidental by the horse, though it may well be in reality as far too many trainers are unaware of not only where it is and what it is doing, but that however it moves, by intent or negligence, the horse is watching. Therefore, repeated, inadvertent movements will soon dull the horse to its presence. He will learn to expect no message from it by its willy-nilly flailing in the air about him.

However, if the trainer is acutely aware of the whip's potential and has made it an extension of his thought, as illustrated through his physical posture and movement, the whip is sharper than any other aid. It compels the horse toward animation and as such, encourages attention and self-expression from the horse. It goes without saying that once the horse is enlivened in this manner, he becomes softer to the physical aids and more receptive to the trainer's thought.

So in the end, it is not the hands that make the horse soft and yielding. It is the whip that finds the softness in the horse for it carries the knowledge and compassion of the trainer.

The Rider's Position

Within each cell of the body there is thought; within each fold of the brain there is sensation. Nowhere do we discover this more graphically than on the back of a horse. Here, the purely mental and physical do not exist separately. Instead, they derive their knowledge from each other and circulate freely to increase the perception of the entire rider. This is the manner in which the horse functions; it is also the manner in which the rider must function in order to be comprehensible to the horse.

So between the brain and the body there is not as much separation as we assume. They each possess the capacities of the other: the body is smart; the brain is sensitive. Reason and judgment are not exclusive to the brain; action and feeling are not properties solely of the body. We also think with our bodies and feel with our brains.

So how does this relate to the position of the rider on the horse? Simply this: the more the body and the mind strive toward the same end, the more the likelihood of mastery. The mind and body are not confined to districts but permeate the entire form that is human. The ideal position of the rider on the horse, therefore, is largely a matter of how well these two are integrated and work in collaboration within the rider.

Most of us come to the horse in a fractured state, thinking and feeling both fear and desire. How quickly the two flit back and forth as we forecast what will happen and remember what did. When the scale is tipped in favor of fear, the mind and body are quick to react; too quick. When desire predominates, the mind and body perceive an illusion and are content to revel in its aura; too slow. Both states are woefully incomplete. The first puts the rider ahead of the horse, the second, behind the horse. There is no balance with the horse.

If we realize that the rider's position on the horse is far more than physical and that the mental must be engaged and allowed to be part of the rider's circulation within himself, we arrive at the nature of flow. This flow is collected within the rider much as we intend to collect the horse within himself without shutting him down. Collection within the rider is made up of many attributes: focus or detachment from outside influences, receptivity to the horse, the ability to emphasize one part of the body without sacrificing the whole, the vision of unity with the horse which is part you, part horse, and finally, the tenacity to settle for nothing less than the enactment of this vision. Harmony is, after all, two or more voices combining to form a third which is neither one nor the other but a composite of attributes from each which have not been arrived at without some degree of sacrifice on both parts; the horse, his liberty, the rider, his grounding.

The Position of the Body

If we begin with the rider's position in terms of his body, we find that if it is correct on the horse, it will in turn suggest correctness to the horse. (The opposite is also true which is why it is of vital importance that the would-be rider be schooled on trained horses.) Position is the aid. In other words, by achieving a correct position on the horse, the rider can refine the conventional aids and rely on the fact that just being there in a state of balance and control will encourage the horse without disturbing him. Being, not doing; an invaluable means of teaching the horse.

Correct body position on the horse is no secret. It consists of the alignment of shoulders directly over the hips and ankles directly under the hips. This is the vertical integrity of the rider. Not coincidentally, it is also the position under which the horse can collect and move in self-carriage. Temporal deviations are permissible as long as they support the horse in his work toward self-carriage and the rider immediately returns to his vertical alignment. This is a skeletal alignment with the muscles, tendons, and ligaments supporting the ongoing uprightness of the body stretched both up from the waist and down from the waist. The core of the rider is low and centered in the abdomen, hips, pelvis, and flat inner thighs to the turned-in knee joint. The breath is slow and from the abdomen. The further away from this core and alignment a body is, the more potentially disruptive it is to the unity of the rider with the horse. The more connected to the core and supportive of vertical integrity, the closer the body is to the horse and the more effective it can become as both receiver from the horse and director to the horse. It is both open and commanding.

The substance of the rider's body when in the ideal position is something of paradox in that it is both rigid and flexible, both bone and flesh. The rigidity consists of the absolute strict adherence to verticality in all gaits and transitions with no part of the body left behind the horse or acting in anticipation of his movement. This is the structure and framework necessary for stillness and unobtrusiveness in the rider. It is the essence of connection to the horse and any deviation puts the rider out of touch. As we strive to collect the horse within his own body and show him balance, we must also center our own bodies within ourselves and within the movement of the horse. Collection within the horse and centeredness within the rider are the same thing. They are the means by which we find each other and give each other a place to be. When the rider's body is not centered within itself, the horse cannot be in a state of balance, let alone enter into that harmonious relationship with us that we so desire. It is incumbent upon the rider to master his part of the balance and for this he not only needs an undeviating frame, but the flexibility to surround and support it.

Flexibility means many things but its existence always necessitates a going away and a retuning, an inflation and a deflation. The two qualities most important to the rider are expansion outward and relaxation inward, the going away and the coming back. Of course the rider never actually goes away but the consistency of his body changes as he expands: it becomes lighter. And the contrary is also true. As the body relaxes, it becomes heavier.

Though the up and down motion is perhaps the most readily recognizable demonstration of flexibility within the rider, it is by no means the sole way in which the body has to accommodate the horse's movement. There are actually six dimensions of the seat and by extension, the rider's body: up to down, back to front, and side to side. This is the way in which the horse moves his back and this is the movement to follow at first and later to influence. Each stride of the horse is composed of these individual motions and as the rider feels the horse's back, he is in turn moved by it.

In the canter stride, for instance, the horse's body moves on a diagonal from outside to inside, from back to front, and by the time the stride is completed, has described an arc, up to down. It is therefore erroneous to aid the horse solely with the outside leg. The natural emphasis of motion on the rider's body begins on the outside, but it doesn't stay there; it moves with the horse's back to the inside with the completion of the stride. It also moves from back to front and from up to down. Sometimes, in an effort to capture an idea or a feeling, we dwell on that idea while the horse moves beyond. Nothing is static in movement and our aids, like music, must flow on and on, as long as movement is our medium of expression.

And so, the rider must also be in a state of permeability, as much as he wishes his horse to be. He must take up the movement within his body. The throughness goes both ways with each partner allowing the other to enter. This is the common ground between us, our new balance, our coinciding centers, and our physical connection.

The Position of the Mind

The position or attitude of the mind can be reshaped just as well as the body though not as easily. The mind has a difficult time staying in one place and projecting to the horse a single, decisive idea. Instead, it gets embroiled in arguments with itself. The very fact that it can do this almost guarantees confusion; the exact opposite of what we want to reveal to the horse.

Before the mind can be expected to behave with effectiveness toward the horse, several conditions must be met. First of all, decision comes before anything else. You must make a conscious, blatant decision that you actually want to be on the back of the horse. It must override all doubts and misgivings that you can conjure up even if it has to put up a false front at times of testing. The more firm your resolve, the easier it will be to master a single course of thought without deviating.

Oddly enough, the decision to ride the horse is most successful when it springs from an emotion: love. When you come to the point where you can do nothing else but, when love for the animal is so compelling, so overwhelming, you have laid the foundation. The mind can then be trained.

To put the mind in the habit of working toward a goal without undermining it, a certain accumulated knowledge of what and what not to do must be acquired. This is the stuff of books and good instructors. Both underline the fundamentals: body position, arena shapes and patterns to be ridden, and a good dose of horse psychology and behavior. By rigorously enforcing these fundamentals over and over again, the rider is expected to gain in confidence through repetition. But repetition for the sake of repetition is not enough. In fact, it is this method of "practice" that shuts down the mind and dulls it to the point where it just has to escape in some other direction, most often to a totally unrelated subject but the one at hand. It is here that confusion arises.

Each repetition must be improved in some way, not merely in technical execution, but in the way in which it is thought of in and of itself and as belonging to something larger. It is this heightened sensitivity that lives and breathes with the horse and the capacity of the mind to create in each repetition something slightly different, something slightly more meaningful. The mind thus maintains interest through change.

Flexibility within the discipline of training is not just necessary to keep the interest of the horse. It is also necessary to keep the mind of the rider focused yet lively. This is not so easy since flexibility and discipline are often at odds with each other, waging war within the rider with each insisting on victory. But it is precisely this interaction of the two that is pertinent to excellence. When the discipline is in place, it actually engenders flexibility. This is about as close to the structure of creation as it is possible to get, no less so simply because it takes place on the back of a horse.

Discipline contains the foundation of knowledge necessary for mastery of a subject. Flexibility is the unique way in which that knowledge arises to meet a given situation in a specific space and at a specific time. It is the flexibility that gives life to the knowledge, taking it off the shelves, so to speak, and enacting its intent. It is the foundation that secures this flight of creation, giving it a reference to return to for validation. Foundation without flexibility is unrealized. On the other hand, flexibility without foundation has no point. Both qualities must be present in the mind of the rider. One without the other is incomplete and tips the scale toward rigidity on the one hand or chaos on the other.

The mind has yet another capacity particularly useful to riders: that of being able to select a single image to project to the horse while actually registering another. This has the ability of an inchworm both stretching forward to the next moment yet always firmly in the reality of the present. This is how the aids work. While asking for the next moment, you are simultaneously assessing and modifying what is underneath you at the time. This is how it is possible to shape and enliven the horse into his ultimate self-carriage. This is also how it is possible for the horse to offer his own unique contribution to the duo. In this way he always has a moment for his own expression before you comment on it. It is when the horse's expression matches your mind's ideal that perfection has been reached. It is possible and it is precisely the control of your thought that makes it so.

And thus, the mind is both rapid in concept yet solid and peaceful in its certainty. And, it is both at the same time. It knows where it is going yet it is always in the same place. In this way, it never gets ahead of itself and even more importantly, never gets ahead of the horse.

The Position of the Emotions

Ah, that much-maligned quality of the human: emotion. It has been blamed for everything from weakness to deception and credited for everything from religious inspiration to the creation of great works of art. We tend to view it in opposing terms, either decrying its lack of intelligence or celebrating its warmth. It is a confusing attribute, to be sure. But is there something finite about emotion, something useful to us in our dealings with the horse?

To begin with, there are only two emotions the horse understands: love and fear. To distinguish them from other human emotions such as frustration, anger, and greed, let us call love and fear the pure emotions. These are the emotions we have in common with the horse. Most often when we deal with the horse we project one or the other to him. Obviously, the emotion of love will go a long way in signifying to him acceptance, comfort, and stability, thereby promoting trust. But how about fear? This is also readily understood by the horse but often with unfortunate consequences. Fear in the horse usually promotes flight or fight and ends any communication before it begins. The horse has only one overwhelming reaction and that is to alleviate his fear in whatever way is open to him. If he is cornered, he will fight. If he is in the open, he will flee. Either way, the rider loses. The horse is no longer accessible to him.

The position of love, therefore, is of fundamental importance when approaching the horse and requires cultivation for it to be manifest. Most people begin with specific love for a particular horse and spend their lives searching for a duplicate when that horse has passed on. Instead, the specific should become the general where love is for all horses, for horse-ness, if you will, or the uniqueness that is horse. Only in this way can love become the long-term foundation underlying all the rider's dealings with horses. And only in this way can the body, mind, and spirit act as an integrated whole. So dispense with the superfluous and return again and again to that motivation which engenders the ideal: love. It is what the horse understands and the place in which he will look for you.

The horse is a great teacher. That being said, it necessitates explanation. The horse can only be a teacher if the position of the rider in all manifestations is both knowledgeable and receptive, strong yet flexible. This is the responsibility of the rider. His body must think, his mind must feel and it must all occur under the auspices of an unqualified regard for the horse. Only when these aspects of wholeness are in agreement in the rider will the horse enter and begin his role as guide.

A Picture of Energy

There is a grave misconception being taught in regard to riding the horse: that to get the horse to go forward, we must squeeze with the legs and that to stop him, we must pull back on his mouth. (So much for the idea of "aiding" the horse!) In terms of energy, this is totally backwards. Regarding what is natural for the horse, this is again totally backwards. And of course, what it says about us in our dealings with the horse, "backwards" is too kind. "Ignorant" would seem to be the better description.

We cannot see energy per se, but we can see and feel the evidence of it. It is apparent in movement and sound. We know that it is the animating force behind our horse's movement and yet we go against energy's natural propensity for flow. "Forward" is a much applauded concept in dressage but its creation and maintenance are usually against the normal path of motion. In other words, we get in the way of movement by not understanding what it needs to exist.

Energy moves. That is what it does. When something is in its way, it diminishes, finds an alternate route, or stops altogether. Knowing this in turn suggests how we should use our aids. If we are in the way through their application, the horse cannot possibly move. This is, incidentally, how we do a down transition or halt: purposely get in the way of the energy. And conversely, if we wish the energy to keep flowing in the horse, we must not get in the way but allow it to flow through us uninterrupted. The horse is not the only one in this pair who must be permeable. We as riders must also allow the energy to flow through us.

In the well schooled horse, energy is self-perpetuating. It flows not only forward but back on an oval path when redirected by the rider. Initiated in the fetlock joints of the horse's hind legs, the energy moves up through the hocks, stifles, hips, and forward over the back and under the rider's seat. Here is where much of the energy stops since it is here that the horse feels the greatest surface of the rider and any "drag" produced by contraction will weaken the forward impulse of the horse.

From the back, the energy continues forward up the neck, over the poll, and down to the mouth and nose of the horse. And here is another stopping place where the energy is turned back via the reins to the rider's hands. Since the hands are closely connected to the eyes, and seeing is given to deception, the hands become arrogant in and of themselves and prefer to act as sole arbiters. When the hands do not reflect what has come before, namely, the character of a particular energy, they act out of context and the probability for continuance of that energy diminishes. In the perpetuation of energy, the hands are turnstiles where the energy is not allowed to escape out the nose of the horse, but is redirected back to the rider and follows a path of hands, elbows, shoulders, down the back, through the seat, down the legs and back to the hindquarters of the horse. Each of these points along the way, whether in the horse or rider, can either allow or impede both the forwardness and the contour of the ride. The rule is: create the energy, then shape the energy. There is nothing more. The creation and the shaping are the two faces of energy.

In order for this path to be maintained, every atom of the horse, has to be in alignment according to his line of travel. Like a current of electricity, there should be no resistance along the way from either horse or rider. In this case, the destination itself is flow with the shape of the horse, not to mention the rider, determining that flow. When both shapes of horse and rider are connected through the rider's grounding and the horse's balance, the energy flows between the two on a new path of circulation.

In order for the energy to circulate then, there needs to be an absolute separation of the aids given by the rider, no matter how small in duration. As the hand comes on, the leg comes off. As the leg comes on, the hand comes off. This is the magician's art performed on the horse: now I'm here, now I'm not. Appearing and disappearing is at the core of continuance. Without appearing, there is no creation of energy but without disappearing, there is no future for that energy. The horse must be inspired, (the "go forward" aids), then shaped, (the "in this manner" aids). And, the aids are continuous but not constant. In other words, the aids are applied in moments, not in large, forbidding increments of time.

In the application of the aids, the tension is always followed by the release and this occurs in fractions of a second, almost never longer. Like an electric fence, the energy is always there but is only palpable when the aids are applied in this alternating manner. The energy will cease if all the aids are applied at the same instant and most often the horse will brace himself against them. The allowance for energy requires a touch there, a touch here, over and over again to guide it along its path. In the most refined sense, the aids are reminders, mere suggestions on how to proceed. They may express the edge of a demand but they are nonetheless quiet and in the ambiance of the particular energy desired.

Energy is malleable. It is the substance of the rider's creation. The particular shape it manifests itself in, however, depends on two seemingly opposite notions: that of movement and that of restriction of that movement and that is where we get into trouble. The impulse itself is not enough. It must have boundary. However, the opposite is true also. Boundary without the impulse of animation is a wall enclosing nothing. The contour of the horse, therefore, has everything to do with the shaping of energy as it is being created. How much space to give the horse back to front is a question of how plastic the horse is and whether or not he is capable of maintaining the desired energy within that space. The shorter the horse horizontally, for instance, the taller he becomes vertically. In order to become shorter, however, he must flex the joints of the hind legs forward under his mass thereby increasing the bend of the haunches which in turn will raise and lighten the shoulders, neck, and head. This is collection but it is also mobility. It is energy traveling uphill in an arc toward the receiving rider and along an uninterrupted path of self-perpetuation back to its beginning and forward to its peak. And round and round it goes with no exit, on a course of infinite possibilities precisely because we have allowed it to flow and to have shape.

When the horse enters the arena, he is defining space. This is more than simply the grid his feet delineate or the pattern of letters that mark his passage. He is, in fact, carving out his own substantial existence by occupying space as he moves through it. The perfection of his movement depends upon how well the rider shapes the energy he is in part creating. Too much hold and the energy will become contorted or cease altogether. Too little and the energy will escape. The collection of the horse under the rider requires a kind of radical middle approach wherein that elusive, invisible, dynamic quality of energy is given life and shape through alternating tension and release, always moving toward the release. And it is the fusion of these opposing impulses in rapid succession that keeps the current flowing and the horse moving toward self-carriage.

The Two-By-Four Lesson

Let me lay out a little path for you. It starts in the gravel driveway, a circle surrounded by a house, indoor, stable, and various outbuildings. It proceeds straight from the driveway and turns right just before the road. It continues on a dirt trail up a hill and past the outdoor arena. At the top of the hill, the path again turns right and proceeds along a tree line separating it from an open field. At the end of the tree line, there is an opening left into the grassy stubble of the field. This is the course followed many times by horses and riders. It is also the path on which I learned something very important about the nature of the horse: that on his own, he will choose to do only those things that fall within his realm of efficient survival. In other words, exertion, except in times of danger or threat, is not within the horse's frame of reference.

Since this was my first horse and I, a mere twelve years of age, was totally unaware of the particular way in which horses act and think, my anthropomorphizing did little except provide the attitude that horses were at least as important as I was, if not even more important. Armed with this attitude was not a bad thing but proved to be woefully self delusional. I was about to learn that not all animals, even those endowed with my undying devotion, felt or thought about life the way I did. My anthropomorphizing was due for a revision, one that included and allowed for the distance of subjectivity on the path toward truth. Just who was this creature who possessed such command over my entire being? What was he thinking and why did he act the way he did, often thwarting my sincerest attempts at union with him? I was about to learn some answers to these questions about the horse and about how the human mind can be adamantly rigid and blind when confronted with the particular world of other inhabitants of this rich planet.

The first few rides on my beloved "Oric" were sprinkled with that exuberance of youth that only diminishes when more subtle perceptions take over. Something was going on but I was so overjoyed at riding my very own horse, that the undercurrents of Oric's intentions were missed altogether. After all, the sun was shining, the path was laid out clearly before me, and I was mounted on the most beautiful horse in the world. Life could not be better.

On the first day of what I would later see as a gradual albeit logical decline in our relationship, everything went fine until we came to the final turn on our journey, the left turn out into the open field. Oric stopped and wouldn't budge. After several minutes of pleading and somewhat unceremoniously using my booted heels on his sides, I gave up, turned him around, and headed back to the barn. I was frustrated but attributed his unwillingness to being tired or having an "off day." No big deal, I thought to myself. Tomorrow would be better.

Day two on my journey was again sunny and warm and boded well for a long ride on Oric. Not giving virtually any thought to what happened the previous day, we merrily proceeded down the driveway and up the hill toward the field. At the top of the hill, however, Oric wouldn't turn right. Try as I might, I couldn't get him to go forward. Nothing worked. My quite limited knowledge at that time, didn't give me any solutions and so as on the day before, we turned around and headed back to the barn.

By day three, the hill was included in our ever shrinking geography. No way would Oric turn right and proceed up the hill. We were left standing at the end of the driveway with no place to go. Well, there was one place: back down the driveway and so that's exactly what we did.

Neither the laws of nature nor spatial awareness had yet begun to penetrate my consciousness. What I did acknowledge, however, was that Oric, at each change of our course, had refused a particular request: turn left into the field, turn right on the dirt trail, turn right up the hill. He was backtracking at each point. In short, he was gaining ground and I, alas, was at a loss as to know what to do. I was even too bewildered to be able to formulate where we would (or wouldn't) go from here. I had not yet begun to put the pieces together even though I had been a participant. Obviously, I had been going along for the ride. My knowledge of normal horse behavior was woefully inadequate.

Day four was again bright as well it should have been. Enlightenment, awakening, epiphany, are all described in terms of light and so it was a fitting ambiance for what was about to happen.

Tacking up went normally as did our emergence into the driveway for mounting and the start of our ride. I had faint hope our ride would proceed without a hitch since the previous three days had been less than stellar. But I mounted nonetheless and asked Oric to proceed down the driveway. Nothing happened. I asked again with my heels, harder than before, and still, no movement. Desperate, I took the ends of the long reins and slashed them over his right flank but again, nothing. This time Oric was ignoring me right from the start. I realized something had to change but had no idea what. At this point, it never occurred to me that it was me that had to change, not the horse.

Also unknown to me was the fact that I was being watched and had been watched each of the previous three days. Mr. Struck, the owner of the farm and a cowboy in word and deed, had secretly been observing my plight from the house and had decided on day four to intervene. As I sat beached atop my dear horse I heard Mr. Struck yell sharply down to me, "Stay there!" As if I could do anything else. None of my attempts at moving Oric were having any effect other than wearing me out. He was adamantly fixed and I was doing all the moving. Something was definitely wrong with this picture.

My bewilderment was soon to change dramatically. Out of the corner of my eye, I saw Mr. Struck race down the steps to the barn behind me, disappear for an instant, and reappear again carrying a three foot long two-by-four. As he trotted toward me, he barked loudly, "Now keep going!" With those words, I felt a lurch forward as Oric, impelled by the resounding smack of the two-by-four on his fleshy haunches, took off at a gallop down the gravel driveway. The first right turn was wide and ungainly but we were on our way up the hill. At the top we scrambled through another right turn and galloped straight along the tree line. If Oric had even a moment's doubt about taking the final left turn, he certainly didn't have time to act on it. We were out into the field before he could formulate his thoughts. The impact of the two-by-four, only minutes ago, was urging him on and I was getting the idea: forward. We spent the next half hour going forward in that inviting field. What heaven. Oric and I were practicing the same thing and beginning to understand the rudiments of horse/human communication. We were in agreement and life was again good. Of course, I would not realize the full import of this event until many years later but the foundation was laid, if only I would take it and run with it. And run with it I did. Poor Oric became a wonderful trail horse, a quick and agile barrel racer, a brave and reliable jumper, and finally, a loyal and trusting dressage mount. What he thought of all this he never did say but I had located his goodness and he in turn encouraged me to pursue what has become a lifelong journey. As for Mr. Struck, he is still, I'm sure, galloping through his days and thinking, if not saying, "Keep going. Keep going."

The horse is a master of space. He uses it to define his position within his community much as in human sports and warfare, the victor is the one who gains ground from the other. With the human, the results are often questionable. With the horse, however, this is not the case. His position confers benefits on the entire group. His gain in space is a means of reinstating peace and stability among herd members. Once this order is established, each horse is quite content to be within his place within the group. This is not to say there are not frequent skirmishes as even horses further on down the line in the hierarchy will try to gain ground from those above or keep their ground from being taken by those below. In the horse's natural habitat, the plains, the dispute is settled without injury. There is plenty of space for the loser to move away. In fact, the leader can be defined as the horse who gets another horse to move. This is knowledge and law to every horse who has ever existed.

So what does this have to do with dressage? Everything. The training of the horse, especially within the demands of dressage, is a systematic theft of the horse's desire to be master of his own space. Each request that we make, each aid that we deliver, tells the horse to move in a particular way. We are constantly telling him to move and thereby reciting the message: "I am the leader of this duo because I am the one getting you to move." This is how the horse views it. Each time the horse acquiesces, he is acknowledging your role as leader. Each time he doesn't, he is attempting to move into that position himself. How well he succeeds or fails depends upon how well and how quickly you read, understand, and respond to each nuance of his expression.

In this narrative, I have attempted to show that the horse can be quite obvious in his desire to win space for himself. At each juncture on my path with Oric, he refused at a particular time, always when there was a change involved; turn right, turn left, movement itself. He had systematically gained ground until he held the ultimate position over me: inertia. What better example of assertion over another than blatant refusal to respond at all?

From this episode, I began to give thought to the horse, not in the sense of what I thought about him, but what was there, apart from me. It became clear that I had committed the ultimate act of disrespect toward Oric and horses in general, based on the assumption that the horse felt the way I did, thought the way I did, and would act according to my wishes. So I began the long process of separation from which wisdom arises. As much as I would wish it were not so, the reality was in difference. Oric was a horse, one I loved dearly, but one who had his own code of operation. It was only when I accepted our apart-ness that I began to understand that the burden was on me to change how I looked at not only the horse but indeed, the whole panorama of creatures that would parade through my life.

And so, the impact of that day long ago deepened my consideration for who I was in relation to the horse. I would come to learn I was neither master nor slave but both: slave to knowledge of the horse apart from me and master of my actions as one member of the herd. The two would prove to be inseparable as both my herd and my comprehension increased. Thank you, Mr. Struck and Oric.

Go Left, Go Right

We all ride two horses: one goes left, one goes right. This is the way in which the horse comes to us and to a greater or lesser degree, the way in which he will present himself throughout his life. There will always be a difference.

To say that a horse is hollow or stiff on one side or the other is a gross oversimplification. To say that he has a good side or a bad side fails to name just what about that side is good or bad. Why do movements going left and movements going right differ so greatly and just how do they differ? Isolating these differences precisely is indispensable to good training and absolutely necessary for the demands of balance placed on the dressage horse. When we take the horse out of nature and insist he move according to the constraints of the arena, we had better thoroughly understand how most horses move most of the time under their own initiative.

To the Left

Most horses, given a choice, will choose to go to the left rather than to the right. This is their natural inclination. It is also their stronger side but this is somewhat of a trade-off since with strength comes diminished flexibility. The positive strength aspect, however, means that the strides are generally longer, covering more ground to the front than when the horse tracks to the right. This in turn leads to a slower, steadier rhythm which is generally pure and more easily sustained. Since the rhythm is slower, there is more time for range of articulation in the joints. With the natural flexion left, the horse's rib cage suspends slightly right in the lateral movements, giving rise to a more even bend through the body. Even the neck, that most flexible area of the anatomy, bends to the left with less distortion and more stability than when bending right. However, it is with less flexibility that it does so. The neck is more likely to telescope forward and downward with a better overall stretch with the nose "slightly" in front of the vertical.

All of these positive aspects, however, have a side which is not so positive. As stated earlier, for each positive aspect there is something less positive occurring and this is not less so in the difficult balance between strength and flexibility. To the left then, we have a horse who is strong, which is good, but when that strength is used against us, strength takes on a decidedly different complexion. The precise areas in which this strength is manifest are in the neck and jaw since these are the last areas to be affected by the circulation of energy before it is rerouted back to the haunches. This is slightly less apparent when bent; more so when moving straight. The trainer will feel the horse harder in his mouth on the left side, less movement of the bit will take place, even the flow of saliva will be less. Often when attempting to soften the horse on the left, the head will tilt down to the outside or the horse will choose to soften backwards, towards the chest rather than outward to the left. It is only by careful balancing into the outside rein that the soft flexion can be achieved.

To the Right

In general, when the horse moves to the right without restraint, he will present a natural flexion to the left in the head and neck. If this natural balance is altered, however, by aligning him throughout his body in the bend right, several other things will happen. He will become faster in the legs which will shorten the stride. He will also raise his poll and shorten his neck. He will attempt to regain his "normal" counter-flexed position by sliding his rib cage to the right, (going against the right leg of the rider), displacing his haunches to the inside and sometimes, becoming uneven in the croup with less time given to the thrusting hind leg, the left, than to the right. The resulting uneven rhythm is the sure sign of lack of balance which in turn indicates a lack of suppleness or strength or both. The right lead canter is also often disunited with the haunches swinging to the outside and switching behind to the stronger left lead.

Though the horse is generally weaker to the right, he is much softer in the hand with the neck flexion often overdone. Stretching the neck forward and to the right is the problem as the horse often seeks to operate behind the hand if the flexion is demanded rather than carefully schooled. In general, the horse going left will resist the action of the bit (the request for flexion) by going above the bit. To the right, he will duck behind the bit. In the former case, he is too much there; in the latter, not enough.

The Legs

In movement, the legs and footfalls of the horse are of critical importance since they are the reflections of what is up above and deviations in tracking can point to problems in conformation or habitual posture. However, conformation is not yet dressage. It is how the horse handles movement that matters and several points can be made about the way in which the horse naturally moves his legs.

Each joint of the leg, whether front, (fetlock, knee, shoulder), or rear, (fetlock, hock, stifle, hip), has an initial range of motion that we as trainers need to increase. There is the back to front action, as displayed in the basic "go forward" gaits, the side to side action, as seen in the lateral movements, and the down to up motion, culminating in the collected movements of piaffe and passage. This would seem to be all well and good and the path to straightness and collection a simple one but it is not, for each leg of the horse is an individual and prefers to move according to its own limitations rather than obey our artificial laws of symmetry. Part of this is conformational, part is habitual way of going, and part, our own lack of keen observation and knowledge as to how to improve the horse. Nonetheless, the horse remains the horse and we must deal with him as he comes to us.

By far, the most dexterous leg of the horse is the left front. It rises up to the apex of the piaffe and thrusts forward in the dramatic reach of the extended trot. It is the least problematic to educate with the exception of its rotation to the right as in the half pass. This is difficult for most horses, possibly emanating from the stronger, more developed left shoulder which "gets in the way" of the swing of the left front leg to the right. The focus here should be not the forward movement of the leg, but the crossing to the left.

The left hind leg is the next most capable leg and in its full development, is the strongest and most able to bear weight. This is why the canter pirouette to the left is easier to keep together than the pirouette to the right. The left hind leg prefers to go straight underneath the body and like the left fore, finds it difficult to move to the right. For the shoulder-in left, this works to the trainer's advantage with the temptation to cross the hind legs almost non-existent. It is a handicap in the half pass right, however, with less magnitude in the crossing.

And now we come to the more problematic legs of the horse and indeed, the more problematic direction, with its inherent difficulties in straightness and even bend throughout the body. Going right is not only a strength and suppleness issue, but a straight one as well.

The right front leg of the horse has a decided tendency to track to the right rather than proceed straight. Often this is accompanied by a rotation of the shoulder and indeed the leg below moves forward and to the right in a kind of half arc. It is as if the horse has to rapidly support the shoulder weight not by advancing forward but by displacing sideways. This, of course, makes the shoulder-in right a challenge but a necessary movement for the freeing of the right shoulder as it has to move to the left. Generally, the reach forward is also more limited as is the raising of the foreleg in piaffe.

And last, and to a great extent least: the right hind. This little renegade is the most rebellious of the four legs and can display several problems at once. The lesser of the problems is that it would rather escape to the left than proceed straight underneath the horse's body. For the leg-yield left this is no problem but for the shoulder-in right, this poses a decided difficulty in carrying ability. Often, this is accompanied by a dragging of the toe, a reluctance to break over quickly and cleanly enough to adequately and efficiently support weight. Moreover, the hock joint of the right hind can display a certain instability as the foot itself is placed to the left but the hock rotates above it to the right. This is particularly noticeable in the walk with the toe moving left followed by the heel moving right once the hoof is on the ground. It is at this time that the hock rotates outward. Between the tendency of the right front to travel to the right and the right hind tendency to travel to the left, the horse, in effect, is in a quasi turn-on-the-center when going right which only illustrates further, the natural crookedness of the horse.

Movement

Of course the horse is composed of far more than neck, head, feet, and legs and in movement to either direction, we can observe a number of other distinguishing features. This being said, we come to the natural order in which the horse's gaits improve.

The first gait to improve is the walk per se as it is the most stable gait and the excitement of impulsion is at a minimum. And it follows that the first side to improve is the left, since it is naturally stronger. Next is the walk to the right with its somewhat reluctant hind leg. In relaxation and hence coordination, the left side is always better in the beginning as evidenced by the greater forward swing of the left hind leg. The right is a little brother by comparison, losing some of its direct forward swing through the displacement of the right hind to the left.

In concept, the trot does not vary considerably from the walk except in terms of straightness. In general, there is a decided increase in crookedness as the gaits increase, with the trot right more variable than the trot left. Unevenness in the croup often appears to the right while the trot left can be perfectly symmetrical and rhythmic to the left. Again, the right hind plays a major role in these distinctions and even to the left, if given a chance, the horse will track slightly to the outside thus displacing the haunches to the right.

Collection in the trot is normally easier to the left as are the extensions which emanate from it but there is a caution here. While the horse is stronger to the left and hence better able to "sit" in the collection, this strength also makes him less flexible so that the movement can become more mechanical, less flowing. To the right there is less amplification of the trot but the quality of the trot is more contained within itself and therefore, in all moving parts.

Sidedness in the horse is always more apparent in the canter, especially when the horse moves on a straight line. With an uncultivated horse, the canter to the right is often impossible and when it does happen, is often disunited with the left hind stepping in to "lead." (Ah, the quirky right hind again!) With the educated horse, differences between left and right will still be present, most often in the amplitude of the stride and the straightness. The flying changes pose a special challenge with most horses changing from weak to strong, right to left, with less difficulty. When the opposite change is asked for, however, the change is often late behind and may even be accompanied by a buck as the horse struggles to get his right hind leg in a position to "lead." (No one out of choice will do what is not easy for himself!)

Inherently, the canter is an unbalanced gait for the horse with his center of gravity shifting longitudinally within each stride as he moves through the three phases culminating in a moment of readjustment, positioning his legs (in the air) for the next stride. There is a lack of "earth time" here that is not found in the walk or trot. It is this lack of being bound to the earth that is appealing to children and more adventurous adults. The canter has the feeling of flying.

Be that as it may, for the dressage trainer, there are the parameters of straightness and symmetry to be produced and many times, not without difficulty. The canter has its own particular shape but within that shape, tendencies often arise that disturb its purity.

Each stride of the canter presents not only a back to front and up to down movement within the horse, but also a diagonal movement from outside to inside. This in turn suggests a kind of arc within the horse's body from outside hind, (the onset of the stride), to inside fore, (the completion of the footfalls), that is not completely straight. The horse places both ends against the middle which is why it is often easier to get a strike-off from a young horse by adopting a quasi-pirouette position. Unfortunately though, this poses problems later on when the horse must be absolutely straight for the flying changes. When bent with the haunches to the inside, the haunches must swing from side to side in order to change to the new inside hind leg. This not only takes too much time but deprives the new inside hind from reaching straight under the mass of the horse where it should be. Impulsion is lost when the horse is not straight.

The Eyes

This might come as a surprise to some, but the eyes of the horse require some special consideration when examining sidedness. They are the first indicators of the thought and emotions of the horse and in a sense, they give rise to movement itself. What the horse thinks and feels comes before his purely physical expression and so it is these capacities we should be "reading" before we examine his movement on our preconceived grids of expectation. And, it is the eyes which reveal whether the horse is thinking or feeling or rapidly fluttering between the two.

Each eye of the horse is capable of expressing a different thought or emotion at the same time. Like the ears, which can "point" in different directions at once, the eyes actually demonstrate the capacity of the horse for focus and distraction, excitement and relaxation, all at once. In addition, they also both receive and express, both taking in and giving out, quickly, and with seamless coordination. As such, they are the indicators of both the thought and the emotions of the horse. Which of these capacities gives rise to behavior is largely up to the trainer.

In terms of sidedness, the eyes are in accord with the difficulty or ease with which the horse moves. Rapid eye blinking, a sign of super awareness, (stress), is most often seen in the right eye of the horse, while the left, even when blinking, is slower and more assured.

Inasmuch as the eyes of the horse can register visual images within almost an entire circle, one would expect a wide range of expression from them. And, they do not have to match in that expression and usually don't. The eyes reflect reaction to images over time and since they are situated at almost opposite poles, no wonder the horse can be in two different worlds at once. He almost physically is.

The Brain/Psychology/Personality (and hence, Behavior)

It is difficult finding a heading for this section since so much of what we attribute to the brain, we see as primarily within the human domain. Animals are somehow different, hence apart, hence unrecognizable as human, hence lower than. It is far too easy to assume that because there is, other-ness there is a difference in value or acumen. Unfortunately, human history is built on just that premise: that when there is more than one, there is always higher/lower, better/worse, intelligent/bestial. There cannot be "other-ness" without a value being assigned and that preference for hierarchy is precisely what diminishes us within the "grander" scheme of things.

We are always thinking in terms of opposites, not wholeness.

The horse, on the other hand, is a creature of integration. What he thinks, he does; what he does, he thinks. There are no ulterior aspects to this animal, no possibility for deception either toward his environment or toward himself. He is whole, connected, in balance. He is not otherwise. That is not to say, however, that he is a creature of simplicity. He is not, as we shall discover when we study him. If we consider the horse in terms of his brain and his body, (polar opposites in human opinion), we find that they are not opposite in the horse. They work together, each possessing the qualities of the other. The brain senses, registers information; the body calculates and measures space. The horse is a vast creature of interdependence, his wholeness, a prototype identical to the larger exterior independent structure he lives within: the herd.

So what does this have to do with sidedness?

To train the horse, we must understand how the horse is structured within his thought, (how he is wired), and what possible outcomes will arise from those innate patterns when the horse is required to change.

Horses vary considerably along a flight or fight continuum but all horses possess both behaviors, albeit in different degrees at different times. The sidedness comes into play in both the uncultivated and the cultivated horse. Our task is to curtail the flight and release the fight so that the horse flows without changes in decision.

What the horse's brain tells him is uncomfortable, he will resist doing physically. In the uncultivated horse, this is of course, more apparent than in the schooled animal where education and clever manipulation on the part of the trainer can "cover" the unevenness between sides. Some of the predictable behaviors are:

- The horse will try to go back to the left or back away on the lunge when he is asked to go to the right.
- The horse will disunite his right canter lead when asked to bring his head and neck into alignment in the bend right.
- The horse will move into the pressure of a leg or whip on the right while being asked to move away from the pressure.
- When faced to the right for mounting, the horse will swing his haunches to the right when asked to remain straight.

If any of these behaviors are familiar, it is because they happen with such frequency and with so many horses that it is impossible not to observe them. And from these observations of physical behavior in the horse, we can infer much about the state of his psychology and to go a step further, what our intervention as trainers will likely lead to.

The brain of the horse is reflected in behavior which can be either refined, if it is a behavior which needs improvement, or changed altogether and replaced with a desired behavior. But, even in the cultivated horse, the original seeds will always be there. What it is natural for the horse to do, he will always do to some extent.

The horse without education displays certain characteristics from the beginning that are endemic to his sidedness. When going left, he tends to be stronger and more assured, which is positive. However, with this strength also comes a certain degree of rigidity and bullishness. He is more apt to fight when moving left than when moving right. On the contrary, the horse moving right is the horse of instinct. He is more sensitive to detail in his environment, less assured, and more likely to display the "flight" reaction. He is quicker instantly, often leading to a sudden bolt.

One of the primary objectives of the trainer is to take what the horse is already and change, modify, and refine the animal so that he can be shaped into a more realized and potent version of himself. And, this is exactly what the process of cultivation leads to: we take those elements that are not so desirable for our purposes and cast them in another and more desirable light, working with the horse to come to a new spin on an old tune, so to speak. And, in the end, we should both be singing the same tune.

In the cultivated horse, the sidedness is still there. Instead of the negative aspects (for us!), when he is alone in himself and behaving according to herd code, however, the cultivated horse becomes the expressive horse having turned his behavior from self-interest to self-fulfillment under our judicious and compassionate guidance. If we are trainers enough, we will take what the horse gives us and turn it to an advantage for us both. And this is the measure of training. The horse moving left has relinquished his strength toward us and has become even more powerful with us. He is more assured of who he is and it is the trainer who has made him certain. He does not fight; he has no need to. The same horse moving right, instead of responding to the details of his environment by flying away, now turns his considerable receptivity onto us and becomes the artist of attention. This is the ultimate balance possible between horse and trainer.

And in the end, we still ride two horses. Through our endeavors as trainers, however, we have become the horse's ally and have helped him become both thoughtful and emotional, calm and excited, in short, balanced between his extremes and by extension, his initial sidedness. Though distinctions remain, there is now no separation within the horse. Between his nature and how it has been carefully cultivated, we have come to reveal the entire horse, relying on his own good intentions to guide us.

The Snake on the Rock

Watching the snake glide over and around obstacles, he becomes a powerful metaphor for balance within himself and balance between himself and his world. Like the rider who must balance not only within herself but with the horse as well, the snake has perfected his balance so that the rock in his path is not so much an obstacle as it is an opportunity for practicing balance and thus the rock becomes the necessity for balance, not the barrier to it.

And just why do we need to balance?

We need to balance because change is constant whether we are the horse, the rider, or the snake, for that matter. We live in a swirl where nothing stays the same for more than a nonce. And, the word "balance" is misleading. It sounds as if we can acquire it, that it is something we can grasp and claim as permanent but this is far from the case. The word should be "rebalance" since that is what we are doing: engaging in constant adjustment.

So just like the snake, the rider must also learn balance, in this case, while on the moving horse. Her balance must now take into account the balance of the animal under her and join it in such a way that it is not disturbing to the animal and secure for her.

All too often, however, the rider balances by anticipating where the horse will be in the next moment and ends up never being with the horse either physically or mentally. Here the rider is ahead of the horse as evidenced by a fierce stare and craning of the neck as she looks where she is going but is never where she's at! The horse is left behind trying to interpret this time warp between him and his rider and guess as he might, is never quite sure of her location.

By contrast, the snake embodies certainty. He does not guess, neither does he anticipate. He knows and is content. And he is content precisely because he has no questions. He does not ask whether it is right or wrong, up or down, enough or not enough. For him, all is as it should be. He is as he should be. And, just being seems to be the key here.

For the rider, this is by and large impossible. Even the highly disciplined mind practiced in focusing on a single idea, has a difficult time accepting the notion of just being. But again, this is precisely where the busy mind should center itself: on being, the balance of being, if you will, for this is what the horse knows, not to mention our friend, the snake.

When the snake enters into this purposeful state, he is at one and the same time absorbing his environment and being shaped by it. He is his centered and elastic self yet a part of all he moves through, adopting its shape and imprinting his own. In this relationship, there is no schism: no individual, no other. There is only the balance of inclusion.

In much the same way, the rider absorbs the movement of the horse but is also adopting a particular shape because of it. The horse too absorbs his rider and is undeniably shaped by her; how well, depends on the understanding of balance between and within. The individual integrity of each will guarantee the success of both. How balanced is that? And how different is it from countless instances of balance in countless guises throughout our lives?

In this way alone, riding is a perfect metaphor for life with its constant demands of adjustment, alteration, and acquiescence. And the effort is always toward that elusive necessity: balance. In other words, how much self, how much other, whenever we are part of a couple, a family, a tribe, a nation, and so on. Of course with the horse as partner, we are further complicating the notion of balance by entering into it with a member of an entirely different species complete with his own intrinsic needs. But perhaps that is part of the magic: finding the common denominator and losing the overbearing "I."

So the picture becomes a bit more complex when we consider the vast number of balances that come into play and must be acknowledged as the need arises. The obvious ones are the ungrounded balance of the rider and the new balance of the horse when mounted. And, (here we go), things get decidedly more involved when we put the two together and send them spinning off into space. And it is precisely the space and the time it takes to occupy that space that pose the difficulties.

When we return to the snake coiled on and around the rock, we can see that the one and the other, the snake and the rock, are in harmony even though they are vastly different. And it is because they have found the meeting of time and space, the balance of change, if you will, for even though the rock doesn't move, it passes through time and even though the snake moves through space, he is still within himself.

And so it should be with horse and rider. The rider doesn't move, though he occupies one place after another. And even though the horse moves, he is the same in the repetition of his strides. So it seems to be this blend of opposites that puts us in balance whether within ourselves or between us and another. But, this blend is never the same, never static, never apprehensible except with something like a quick sidelong glance as we become not there but here, and here, and here, always softly changing. How good of the snake to show us this; how good of the horse to carry us through.

Training vs. Conditioning

The measure of a trained horse rests in the choices he makes.

If this statement is indeed true, then much of what passes for training is not training at all, but conditioning. To understand the differences, we need to examine each in terms of assumptions about the horse and our goals for him, from onset to achievement. In other words, where is the horse when we approach him and where is he when we leave him?

What we as trainers assume about the horse is largely responsible for how he will end up being presented. If we assume his limitations, he will show that. If we assume his possibilities, he will also show that. It is an example of the old self-fulfilling prophecy that what we expect, will occur largely by our censorship or our permission, our exclusion or our inclusion, for it is by thought that events occur, not by happenstance.

So what do we believe about the horse?

As trainers, it is incumbent upon us to believe that the horse is a sensate creature, capable of independent thought, and that he is possessed of his own particular view of the world and his place in it. As such, he is precious and deserving as are all creatures who display the "animate urge." To the trainer, the horse is a creature to uncover, not bury under misconception and fruitless supposition.

The conditioner, on the other hand, while recognizing physical response from the horse, wants a measurable reaction each time a prescribed "cue" is given. In other words, while he allows for the physicality of the horse, he uses it to contain and predict the response owing to his view of the horse as limited, containable, finite. As such, the horse's responses are predictable, controlled, and rote. Diluting the horse down to this type of "acceptable" behavior smacks of the laboratory rat learning to press one of three levers to receive his reward: an M & M! Conditioning is not yet training.

In addition to primary beliefs about the nature of the horse, the trainer must also have knowledge and hence belief that the horse is capable of language, both in receptive and expressive capacities, and that communication relies on both he and the horse using that same language for purposes of understanding each other. To veer from that assumption would be to demean the horse and believe that he had no capacity for language. Nothing could be further from the truth, however, since he possesses and displays nothing less than the sophisticated language of time and space, thus eclipsing our feeble attempts at capturing the "life" of language; its breath, if you will. With the horse, no translation is necessary. His language is as direct and precise as sunlight.

For the trainer then, the horse's receptive language leads to his expressive language which is somewhat of a signature of each individual horse. But for the conditioner, self-expression is the enemy. He is often not able to gauge that fine line of distinction between rebellion and expression and sometimes punishes unjustly which ultimately leads to "lock-up," or, the extinguishing of any and all behavior, in this case, forward movement. The conditioner denies the reciprocal quality of language and forces it to work in one direction only: from him to the horse.

In addition to differing psychological beliefs of the trainer and the conditioner, there are also primary philosophical differences between the two approaches to working with the horse.

The aim of training the horse is communication. This in turn entails a rather sophisticated and subtle vocabulary of weight, pressure, glance, and especially, thought. Training the horse presupposes a great deal about the horse: that he can enter into the training process itself without ill effect, that he is a vital part of that process and as such, should participate in it, that he had something to contribute to the "quality" of the outcome, and that, if what he has to say is not incorporated into the process, it just isn't training.

By contrast, in the process of conditioning there is communication occurring yes, but it runs one way. Since the aim of conditioning is control, the response of the horse is severely restricted to only those responses which can be measured. When those boundaries are exceeded, the conditioner has not succeeded in imposing enough control and so will escalate aids until the horse becomes reliably mechanized.

And of course when the aims are so different, the responses are correspondingly different also. And there is a very large branch in the road here between the trainer and the conditioner. In general, (and it is true that many of these practices dovetail), the trainer is looking for a response which demonstrates that the horse had understood a connection: that between the request and his answer to it. This response could include any number of acceptable behaviors. The fact that there is behavior at all, means the horse has understood a kind of causal relationship.

Not so with the conditioned horse, however. His response is preordained in the conditioner's mind and there is only one he will accept. This is the "trick" mentality that depends for its success on bribes, (reinforcements), or "cues" to obtain a desired behavior. However, once the "trick" has been completed, the conditioner will have to repeat the cue over and over to elicit the "trick" once more. Hardly the kind of elevated communication one would hope for, and still we persist. So what is the appeal of the conditioning process itself?

Perhaps our need for entering further into experience prompts us to say the same thing over and over again, as if frequency assures message or strength can ever outweigh potency. Our identity, our "raison d'être," our very core, calls out to be recognized, to be accepted, to be fed like a noisy hatchling in a nest. We need this validation and just perhaps, we believe the horse recognizes us, (and hence obeys us), only because we nag him at every opportunity, asserting our message over his response, if any response could ever rise from underneath the barrage we assault him with in the name of assertive "aids."

While this may be the reason, it can never be the excuse for ignorance and this is precisely where the conditioner finds himself: at the mercy of his own assumptions about the horse. He can only work with the horse insofar as his assumptions allow and of course these limitations are reflected in the dullness of the horse. No matter how obedient, the enthusiasm is lacking. And, it is precisely the conditioner who deprives the horse of choice and ends up shutting him down to the point where response becomes tediously predictable and lackluster.

But, back to the response of the horse.

When the horse acts on account of being trained, he does it by himself. This is to say that the horse has learned and is using nothing less than language to show understanding and in this case, compliance. When he acts on account of being conditioned, however, he does it only when he is told to do so and then, must be constantly prompted and pressed to maintain a behavior. Again, it goes back to who the person with the animal is, and what techniques, standards, bodies of knowledge, disciplines, and ultimately, beliefs, that person operates under. There is no escaping it. You cannot be who you are not, at least, not with the horse. He will always present you honestly and without exaggeration. There is no hiding here.

And so we have come full circle from belief, to aim, to outcome, and back to belief again. And in the end, it is how we consider the horse that determines what we strive for and what we ultimately achieve.

For the conditioner, it is fundamentally the western "man against nature" polarity being displayed with the horse not so much acting as being acted upon. Control is overwhelmingly important to the conditioner, control of the "other," that is. This, of course, places all creatures below the human in ability and by extension, value. And make no mistake, belief does determine the quality of your work with horses, even down to the smallest single-time aid. The mere closing of a finger consists of a dead-end or a hint of possibility; it is all in the way it is done as the way dictates the who behind it. And the horse can tell. He is discriminate and non-prejudicial.

In the "man against nature" world, the horse always loses precisely because he is not man. He must be put somewhere, made to fit into the scheme of things and most often, he is relegated to slave or pet, neither category terribly desirable for any living creature since both undermine the sovereignty of life. And so the conditioner has created a kind of artificial, hierarchal, and simplistic view of the world with himself at the center by virtue of his superior "reason." Anyone with even limited insight, however, can see the fallacy of this one-dimensional thinking simply by an examination of: man's past, man's present, man's motives, man's family. Not stellar examples of the glory of man by any means. Quite the opposite. It is furthermore not difficult to conclude that man is not a negotiator any more than he is comfortable with the notion of freedom. It is just too much not him for him to accept, unless he is forced to.

Yet, it is precisely these two qualities which are necessary in order to be a trainer. First is the ability to negotiate, i.e., to move, to give, to change. Second is the ability to operate within freedom; of thought, of selflessness, of service.

If this sounds like the trainer undergoing his own training before he undertakes the training of the horse, it is so. And the horse will always be the final judge as to whether that training had been completed or a refresher course is in order. The trainer is always en route. The horse always knows where he stands.

There is one glimmer of hope, however, and it is the vision of the horse in self-carriage. That it has been an attractive idea at countless times throughout the centuries and in countless places is not surprising. It embodies that appeal that heaven alone has: the all-powerful that is at the same time light and ephemeral.

What is surprising in dressage, however, is that self-carriage in the horse is not more evident. Currently it is not part of any training system or show ring requirement and has all but disappeared from print and conversation; a most disturbing reality.

If we are to accept that the trainer deals with the horse's sense of self and that the trainer discovers appropriate venues for self-expression within the horse, then the logical outcome should be ever more frequent moments of self-carriage. But alas, when the response has been conditioned rather than cultivated, the outcome is predictably mechanical. And the resulting lack of joyful expression in the horse is nothing less than an abomination of nature.

But again, conditioning is not yet training and it is only the trained horse who is frequently in self-carriage. And this self-carriage is an unmistakable collaboration of opposites with the freedom of the horse occurring precisely because he has learned to maintain shape by himself. Would that we could do as much. Now that would be training!

"Starting Shaman"
A Journal of Beginning

Introduction

There is an immediacy present in training the horse that is never within writing about it. The formality of writing itself and the necessary reflection and deliberation that accompany it, while many times uplifting, nevertheless can undermine its sense of presence. Not so with training the horse.

It was my intention with this piece, to make the writing as close as possible to the training, hence, the journal format. If I could have had pen and paper with me in the arena, that would have been the ultimate test, albeit, a totally impractical one.

As it stands, the close proximity of the writing to the training uncovered for me one truth: that no matter what the knowledge or foundation of the trainer, the trainer is constantly changing and adapting, modifying to meet the needs of the moment. The pen could never hope to keep up with this complexity that is horse; nor perhaps should it even try.

It is in this spirit that the following rendition is offered.

Preface

Educating the young horse is rather simple, but never easy. It requires from the trainer a knowledge of where he is ultimately going with the horse, and a knowledge of the means by which he can get there. It also requires that the trainer be flexible enough to accept small attempts by the horse but never overface him and hence, spoil his willing nature. On the other hand, the trainer must be unrelenting in adhering to the sound principles of training and not compromise his ideals.

For the trainer then, the starting of the young horse is nothing less than an occupation of great creativity and near-obsessive concern. For the horse, we can only hope that what lays ahead serves to give him the means to harmony and expression within himself. What glorious promise.

Thursday, August 28, 2004
Shaman's owner and I loaded him into the trailer for the fist time with no problem. It was interesting to watch as he explored before acquiescing. First one foot went onto the trailer floor, then back out, then both front

feet went on, and back out again. When we added the tapping of the whip on his croup, it was a short time before he walked on slowly and with no fuss. The whole ordeal took about ten minutes.

Lesson one will take place tomorrow. Among other things, a big priority for Shaman will be learning to yield his head and neck forward and down. With his Friesian height and conformation, he can easily escape influence by simply stretching upward.

Friday, August 29, Lesson 1

Shaman had his first full lesson today and was introduced to quite a lot including the foundation of our work together: go forward, stop, give.

We began in the cross ties with which he was already familiar. Picking up his feet was not a big problem except for his rear hooves with which he had a tendency to argue and threaten. (We would see the same behavior on the lunge later on.)

First time experiences came next. Saddle cloth, saddle, and tightened girth went on in short order. (Curious boy that he is, he was more interested in the halters and leads hanging within reach than he was disturbed by anything I was doing.)

Next came the bridle, (over the halter for now), again with no problem. His first reaction to the bit was not an unusual one. He repeatedly and boldly opened his mouth as if the bit were an annoyance he could get rid of. He was by no means afraid of it so we proceeded with the lunge line run through the inside snaffle ring and hooked to the girth. We headed to the arena for the first formal training session.

The first few lessons for a young horse are all about barriers. His normally infinite availability of space in which to move will now be seriously limited. (Shaman has already just experienced confinement in the form of the stable, cross ties, saddle and girth, bridle, and lunge line.) Now he will experience new barriers in the open arena.

Beginning on the left, we walk in small concentric circles as if I am leading him but always with me as the center of his world. He is quite distracted by the new sights but we keep moving until by closing my fingers on the lunge, I can get a momentary recognition of me from him. Little by little, I am being included in his broad attention, if only for brief instants. When these "instants" are sufficient, I send him with the whip paired with the universal "cluck" further away from me onto a larger circle and we again begin our tour of the arena, only less expansive this time. When he is at a distance from me, it is vitally important that his ground covering is limited by the lunge, and that his focus includes me. If it does not, we go back to the "leading" stage. In Shaman's case, we are ready to go on.

Shaman's receptive vocabulary now contains the "cluck," meaning "move on," and we will now enter the word (and concept) "whoa." This is best done on our small circle where enforcement is possible. If the space between us is too large, the message will be lost.

It is now time for Shaman to understand that there are two ends to the lunge whip and that by their position in relation to him, they mean two different things. The butt end of the whip controls the "whoa;" the lash end of the whip controls the "move on." When the butt end of the whip is placed in front of him, it makes a barrier. Conversely, when it moves away from him, it opens a door. When the lash end of the whip moves behind him it means "go forward." When it is in a neutral position behind the trainer, it gives the message to maintain; not go faster, not stop. Shaman is already beginning to learn this "positional" vocabulary and respond appropriately. He watches the whip intently. When he maintains what he is asked on his own, I surrender the whip behind me in the neutral position. I only make it appear when he needs a message. At this stage, its appearance always accompanies a verbal direction. We reverse so that both sides are treated.

Saturday, August 30 and Monday, September 1, Lessons 2 and 3

Shaman's circles on the lunge are now round with no "points" nearest the gate. He is also learning to stay an even distance away from me, always taking up the slack in the lunge line. This translates as "always go toward the bit" and prepares him for what he will be doing under saddle. He is now walking and trotting in equal circles around me as I change position in the arena.

During the second lesson, a long outside side rein was introduced on the lunge. This new barrier induced a lot of exploring with his head and neck as he attempted to find just where he could be comfortable within this new restriction. By today's lesson, Shaman had learned how to "give" in the poll and jaw at the walk; not yet at the trot, however. When the increased energy of the trot was added, it was much more difficult for him to understand the "give" to the bit. That should begin to happen in one or two more sessions.

Work in-hand was started in the second session both on and later off the lunge. What was expected of Shaman was a few sideways steps in both directions with both front and hind legs crossing, inside over outside, in preparation for the shoulder-in. Yielding away from the whip with both shoulders and haunches is many times difficult for a young horse, especially in the shoulders. This posed no problem for Shaman, however. I increased the difficulty by requiring that he keep going in his rotation around me. Both front and hind legs crossed with no apparent glitches in either direction so his sidedness, at this stage anyway, seems to be a non-issue. His response to the whip and the bit was so good yesterday that today he was also worked in-hand with just the bridle reins. From the rotations around me, we now added a few crossings on a straight line, then back to the circle. He is already beginning to understand the elements of the shoulder-in, which is where we are headed.

Today there was no "face-off" from Shaman on the lunge which there had been yesterday when going to the right. The meaning of "forward" is beginning to sink in as he becomes more comfortable in his mind and body and with what is asked of him.

Tuesday, September 2, Lesson 4

At this point something should be said about bridling. It is ultimately an act of trust between the horse and trainer and as such, provides a measure of how well the relationship is proceeding.

On the first encounter with the bridle, the halter remained on and the bridle was slipped over it. In that free time between the restraint of the halter and the restraint of the bridle, horses often try to leave the premises. They are very clever about finding the "open door" so to avoid this, the first bridling is always done over the halter with a cross tie attached to the halter on the right side. In Shaman's case, there was no attempt to leave so in the second and third lessons, the halter was rebuckled over the neck as a precaution and the bridle, put on without the halter underneath.

Today we pushed the trust factor a little further. I was not disappointed. The bridle reins were first placed over his neck, then the halter was removed completely. In that time between halter and bridle influence Shaman remained quiet and the bridling itself went without incident.

Lungeing also progressed smoothly. Shaman has begun to lighten on the line at the trot which is a go-ahead for me to shorten the outside side rein, demanding a greater flexion in the jaw and poll. Initially in the trot left, Shaman went against the bit, thrusting his neck up and out to its extremity. After several times being brought in and worked in sideways steps with head and neck stretched down, he was able to take this position out onto the lunge at a trot. His "give" response is taking hold. He is beginning to understand how to release the pressure himself through flexion of his jaw and poll. Traveling to the right proved a bit more difficult for him, (as it does for most horses), but he finally came into the *ramener* position at the trot and we ended the lungeing at that point with much praise.

Work in-hand continued with the rotations around me in both directions. To the right he is already doing a passable shoulder-in on the straight line. To the left, however, he is still strong so we focus on greater softening.

The next step in Shaman's education is to position him at the mounting block, which is why it is so important for him to begin the work in-hand as early as possible. He must understand how to move his haunches and his shoulders away from pressure and thereby straighten himself. He must also understand the "give" to the hand, not to mention the concept of immobility. When his responses are correctly in place, he is ready to be "worked at the halt" in preparation for mounting. In Shaman's case, no "work" was needed since he stood straight and quietly without moving. This will probably not always be so as he will soon try evasion by swinging his haunches away from the mounting block. Today, however, we are ready to proceed to the actual mounting.

The first time the horse feels a foot in the stirrup is also a test of mutual trust. Neither of us should be fearful or confused. I am very slow and deliberate as I raise myself above him, pause for a moment, and lay over the saddle. In this position I pet him over his belly, flanks, and haunches, telling him in a low, slow voice what a "good boy" he is. He responds by turning his head and neck to the right to look at me and turns forward again, lowering his neck and head. I slip down to the ground, go to his head, stroke his neck, and again impress upon him what a "good boy" he is.

And this is how uneventful it should be.

Wednesday, September 3, Lesson 5

All work with the horse should progress toward self-carriage. This is the trainer's message to the horse: "You know how, now do it yourself." In essence, the trainer teaches, then backs off and allows. The quality of the training therefore consists of how little the trainer does, not how much. Intervention should be limited to modification.

Shaman was much more forward on the lunge today and therefore stronger in the hand. Before the side rein was attached on the outside, he even broke into a canter; a gamboling, legs akimbo, head-in-the-air rendition of the gait. After the rein was attached, he immediately came down onto the bit, even in the trot. Not so to the right, however. It took some time before he came down and stayed for more than a stride or two. Since he offered canter left, I asked for canter right, got it, went back to the "round" lesson at the trot, and ended the lunge work there.

Work in-hand today proved the stage for some serious resistance. It is true that once the horse thinks he knows the rules, whether in the arena or with his herd, he will attempt to reposition himself in the hierarchy and test those rules, seeing if he can raise himself up a notch in the pecking order. Just so with Shaman. In the rotation right, he attempted to rear up against me twice when I increased the demand of right shoulder over left. Fortunately, he didn't get away and we proceeded without stopping until he made one complete rotation, right shoulder over left shoulder.

Up until today, we have been working within the horse's emotion of tranquility with requests for "more," staying within that parameter. Today, however, I have increased the intensity of my demands in two instances because of what he presented me with, namely, his unilateral decision to break into the canter on the lunge, and his also unilateral decision to rear up against me in the work in-hand right. In the first instance, I responded by insisting on another cater left, and after we reversed, the canter right. In response to the rearing, I became the mountain lion momentarily and demanded the crossing with a "do or die" attitude. Once I got what I wanted, the emotional level immediately returned to one of tranquility and praise. Shaman was again content to be "number two."

Despite today's little pushing of the boundaries on Shaman's part, he quickly returned to a state of eager acceptance, (horses not known for carrying grudges), and we proceeded to the mounting block. As in the previous lesson, he stood quietly and straight as I lifted myself in the stirrup and lay over the saddle, patting him as before. I included patting the saddle flap for "startle reaction" response, got none, and slipped down. The second time up, I made the instantaneous decision to swing my right leg over Shaman's back and actually sit astride him. He stood perfectly quiet, craned his head and neck around to the right, and smelled my boot; a perfect reaction in the course of training.

Tomorrow, Shaman will have been here a week. Time for a day off so he can think about what he has learned within the comfort of the herd.

Friday, September 5, Lesson 6

This begins Shaman's second week here. The work on the lunge is progressing steadily with more expression in the trot and little forays into the canter. There were a few face-offs on the right today but the lunge whip on the right shoulder convinced him to continue on to the right. Since the side rein was shortened, he has come into position sooner and stays longer.

The work in-hand today went extremely well with the rotation right actually better than the rotation left. Horses sometimes are like rusty screws. It takes moving them back and forth a few times to loosen them one direction or the other.

Since there has been no problem with Shaman accepting me on his back, we began some work at the halt in the *ramener* today. Putting the horse in *ramener* or onto the bit is something Shaman has already been practicing from day one through the lungeing and the work in-hand. In bridling, leading, intermissions between changing sides, and any other time I am near his head, I ask him to give to pressure. This consistency and frequency on my part will lead to his understanding *ramener* in work under saddle, which is just what he did. When I closed my fingers, it took him a second or so to get the idea, but he dropped his head and neck and began moving the bit in his mouth. Of course he didn't stay there long but we repeated the action half a dozen times and with each request, he responded correctly.

Something should be interjected here on the proper time for the trainer to release his fingers. It is not after the horse has given in the jaw and poll. Then it would be too late and the horse would have no reward as his act toward releasing would be met by a closed fist. Instead, the trainer must make mini-releases as the horse is giving and going down. Strung together, these releases are the vocabulary of communication with the horse, allowing the trainer to put the horse's head in any position he wants. By using them often and with precision, the horse is shown the way to self-carriage. When he feels pressure, he reacts by giving in to that pressure. When he feels no pressure, he learns to stay there by himself. It is that simple.

Saturday, September 6, Lesson 7

Today we dealt with the "unfamiliar object" response. The lawn mower parked next to the arena provoked the "stop, look, and snort" behavior. After the whip told him to go on, each circle on the lunge shrunk toward me when he passed the lawn mower. Once he would trot past it in a controlled shy, we stopped and I led him over to it. His message to me was, "OK, I'll walk toward it, but you first." It must have been quite a picture, me at 5'3" leading a reluctant 16.1 hand horse with him peering over my shoulder at the scary object. After he examined the lawn mower we resumed lungeing. He was light again and immediately round to the left; not so to the right. When the horse has a difficult time relaxing in the head and neck on the lunge, rather than shorten the side rein, I prefer the "tete-a-tete" method whereby the horse is told in intimate fashion, that you would prefer it if he would lower his head and neck. The work in-hand in rotation around you with the horse moving both hips and shoulders is the place for this and usually serves to improve the lungeing.

The work in-hand went from the rotations to some steps to the side in shoulder-in position. In addition, we have been adding small circles in both directions to reinforce the "and, walk on," and "whoa" responses which I will need to have in place for the mounted work.

Today was an important day for Shaman since he took his first steps forward under saddle. They were hesitant and directionless and began from moving backward, but they did go forward. He halted twice when asked, more from the voice than the legs and hands but at this point in his understanding, that is normal.

Let me say here that the requirement to move on also necessitates the horse moving forward in some kind of shape and that shape is round. When the young horse is introduced to this from the beginning, he learns to associate one with the other. Forward means round; round means forward. In this way, impulsion is always paired with lightness. This sidesteps a possible issue often encountered after a year or so of training: the horse will go forward but not without a thrusting up and out with the head and neck. When he is then asked to come into *ramener*, he will lose impulsion or stop altogether, the two concepts of forward and round existing as opposites in his mind. Associating them in the young horse's training right from the beginning avoids conflicts later on and besides, it is nothing less than the enactment of our precious vocabulary; best teach it from the first.

Our next step, from the freshly established halt, will be to use our friend the small circle to put some direction into Shaman's forwardness. The small circle is something he knows already from the lungeing and the work in-hand so the transference will be easy for him. It will also introduce the effect of the outside rein which he will feel as the outside boundary and learn to give to as he has on the lunge and in-hand. The inside rein will function more as a leading rein at this time to get him into the circle and my weight will maintain the circle once he has entered it.

Monday, September 8, Lesson 8

Circles, circles, circles. What would we do without them? They teach the horse to arrange and align his body within a balanced and connected shape. They teach him he has an inside bend and an outside bend. They flex his joints. They make him available to us.

Under saddle today I was again reminded of how the balance of the horse changes under a rider. Our first circles were hesitant, not round, full of stops and starts, and several times a hind leg would buckle. Shaman is very willing though and his "non-accomplishments" are merely unfamiliarities and questions of whether or not he has understood correctly. They ask the question: "Is this really what you want?"

To begin the under saddle lesson, I prefer to not have to kick or overdo the legs to get the horse to move on. I would be asking him to respond to something he doesn't understand yet: the pressure of the rider's leg. Instead, I turn the head first one way, then the other to purposely unbalance and unlock him. He will invariably take a step in one direction or the other and here is my chance to proceed in the walk.

We began with circles to the right, my goal, to have Shaman "walk on." He took a few steps, halted of his own accord, and became locked on the spot. I then dismounted and worked him in-hand briefly to emphasize the "and, walk on" command. I paired the touch of the whip with my voice and he walked on until I asked him to halt. (For connection, the whip touched him where he would feel my leg when I was aboard.)

I remounted and on the first request to "walk on," Shaman understood and forward we went. The connection was made. The halts were still coming from him so my next goal was to get one directed by me, which wasn't easy since he had to take enough steps forward for me to be able to prepare him. Finally I had the opportunity and he came right into my lightly restraining aids. We walked on again, after much praise, and repeated the exercise once more to the right and twice to the left and I dismounted.

The roundness in the horse that I ask for right away is not because the horse should be "on the bit" at some further date, but because he should be with me right now and the position of "on the bit" is an indication of this. This is not a meeting for the future, but a position in which we can communicate right away and one in which my requests can remain civilized and polite, celebrating the great sensitivity of the horse. When Shaman is round, he gives up his instinct and trusts that I will keep him from harm. It is a position of relaxation for the horse and a place where I can influence him positively… and the conversation begins.

Tuesday, September 9, Lesson 9

If I wanted the horse to simply go forward, it would be easier than him having to figure out how to move into pressure. When he feels the closed fingers, his first reaction is to stop or slow. It takes awhile for him to figure out that "go forward" also means "make contact." This is the essence of dressage, however, so teaching the concept of "go forward, be round" right from the beginning actually is faster for the horse than teaching one at a time. They should be more closely associated in the horse's mind than is generally thought of or practiced. When the request to go forward is given, the horse must immediately go toward the bit, seeking the contact himself.

With a young horse like Shaman, not only is moving forward a balance problem under the rider, but the fact that as he attempts to move, I also ask for him to be on contact, is a puzzle right now. To him, it is as if I am saying, "move, now don't move." If the aids are delivered quickly and with the precise intensity, however, it won't be long before he figures out that "forward and round" are essentially the same thing.

Today we went forward under saddle several times without the tap of the whip. Shaman is beginning to understand the first meaning of short, quick leg pressure, which is to go forward.

At this point in Shaman's training, the work in-hand is invaluable for teaching, reinforcing, and reminding him of the basics I am trying to get him to understand. Since the "and, walk on" has been introduced both on the lunge and in-hand, the message has already been planted in Shaman's mind. All he has to do is generalize it to being asked for under saddle. This is not so easy for the horse to do, however, since the rider on his back is an overwhelming distraction to him. So, we alternate between asking for it under saddle and immediately asking for it in-hand to remind him and help him make the transfer. This works very well and also has the added benefit of exposing Shaman to more frequent mountings, more frequent "whoas" and "walk-ons," and especially more frequent and varied opportunities to see that though I change, (from on the ground to on his back), I really do not. My messages and manner toward him are always the same. In this way, he begins to include me in his reality much as he does another horse who may change his position but never his message: "I am your friend. Let's hang out together." Security to the horse is the ability to impart that message to him.

Wednesday, September 10, Lesson 10

The use of the whip has now become an important part of the work under saddle. Shaman is still unsure of going forward into the walk and staying there. He will move off from the legs and voice but will stop after three to four strides.

Shaman's reaction to the whip, (used either behind my leg or on his flank), is no greater than to leg and voice alone but to lighten my legs, the whip in conjunction with them will maintain the walk. At the same time though, we are also always seeking to lighten the aids, (and use them less frequently), so that Shaman responds to less and less; not a simple language for either rider or horse.

The whip is an interesting aid and one that each horse responds to differently. Some will instantly respond with movement, some will lock up against it, and a few will hesitate, then move. In Shaman's case, the whip has little if any "inspirational" effect but we will continue using it until he becomes sensitized. This breakthrough relies for its success on a cumulative effect and the increase in its intensity. It is mandatory that its action ceases immediately when the horse gives a little extra thrust forward in his movement. It is at this point that he is beginning to understand that the whip will stop if he keeps moving. This pattern may have to be repeated dozens of times but eventually the horse will get it and move on at the merest indication from the whip.

Shaman finally moved into "his' walk under saddle today. Both the haunches and the shoulders were swinging forward, the back was moving from side to side under my seat, and for the most part, he was round and softly mouthing the bit. He is learning to go into the hand, to trust the hand, and to be shaped by its influence.

It should be mentioned here that knowledge of the grade of the arena can be put to good use when dealing with the hesitant horse. The arena we are working in has a two-foot grade from one long side to the other so when working at "A" on the short side, half of the circle the horse is making will be going downhill and half will be going uphill. To make it easy for the horse, forward movement is asked for when the downward slope assists him. The halt is asked for when he has to climb. The test will come when we can reverse what is natural for him to do.

Shaman is now half done with his month here: twenty lessons within thirty days. He has come quite far in a short period of time with no major setbacks. The goal for the second half of his stint will be to trot under saddle on 15 and 20 meter circles and to go large at walk and trot. Whether that goal will be accomplished or not is secondary to his further understanding of "forward and round." That and only that is the foundation underlying the perfect horse.

Second Half

Thursday, September 11, Lesson 11

Sometimes the simple act of making a statement causes that statement to become a reality and so it was today with Shaman's first steps of trot under saddle. The plan was not necessarily for today but Shaman peeked in on my thoughts and acquiesced at the second request. It's true that horses have a keen receptive ability and the more I practice sending thoughts, the more I see how the horse actually depends on my mind for direction. It is the most powerful of all aids.

It is interesting to note that Shaman was much easier to keep at the trot than he was at the walk. Impulsion is a definite ally here. His trot was as big and bold as it is on the lunge and his balance improved with the flow of forwardness.

Today involved another of those moments when each of you relies on trusting the other: the transition from walk to trot. It is much like swinging the right leg over a horse's back for the first time. Almost anything can happen; most of the time, nothing does. If the horse has been prepared carefully from the ground, his reactions can be predicted with some surety though there is always the chance of the unforeseen making a surprise appearance. With Shaman, he took the new request with aplomb, as if he had been asked many times before. What a good fellow.

Sunday, September 14, Lesson 12

Today was a deja vu experience with Shaman as I watched him struggle with his balance in deep mud and hoof-sized puddles. I recalled working another young horse, Tejon, under the same conditions and his aversion to going forward, even at the walk. The same was true for Shaman today. The walk was a crawl and there was no possibility of getting the trot so I turned off the "achievement" button and contented myself with the "frequency of repetition" button instead. This is a hard thing to do but the "achievement" would not have been worth it since I would have had to use quite a bit of force to get the trot and risk scaring Shaman which would neither be fair nor productive. His good nature and willingness are too important to compromise.

One of the most difficult things to learn when teaching the horse is: how much is not enough and how much is too much. Error in judgment at the most could be dangerous and at the least, unproductive. It is only through a thorough and general knowledge of methodology and a particular knowledge of that horse that an accurate judgment can be made and hence, an apt request be made of the horse. Mistakes in this can be costly and frustrating to both the horse and the trainer so a quick change of mind (expectation) is necessary. Know when to push; know when to back off. It is the process, the doing that is important, not the end. This is where the horse is already and the kind of mind he comprehends.

Monday, September 15, Lesson 13

Horses are emotional creatures and I often find that the structure of a training session consists in raising the emotions and lowering the emotions in order to communicate my message to the horse. We are still having some resistance to the "go forward" request so by the time we got to the right side in lungeing, I decided it was time to chase the horse, let him slip and slide in the muddy arena, and not let up until "forward" was the first thing on his mind. It didn't take long for his emotions to escalate, his head to come up, and his movement to accelerate. He was "heightened." That was the lesson for today. After spending his energy he quite readily came down and round while still going forward though without the speed. We stopped when this was maintained for half a dozen circles and went on to the work in-hand.

The under saddle work today was unspectacular though Shaman was a bit spent after the lungeing. I asked once for the trot, didn't get it, (not even an acceleration at the walk), and decided to go back in my demands and be content with halt to walk to halt to walk transitions, now on a larger, 20 meter circle. He is still hesitant in his walk and doesn't unlock his body under me. When he does, however, it feels like what my imagination tells me it would be like to ride a camel with large, slow, undulating waves underneath me. He definitely has the Friesian movement.

I should mention here that the insistence on roundness does to some degree get in the way of forwardness until the horse forms the habit of meeting the bit not as something to back away from but as something to embrace and go with, (not restraint but shape). A young horse has trouble acting on these seemingly contradictory directions. Little by little though, I have to content myself with knowing that the foundation is being put in place and that it is only a matter of time before Shaman "clicks on" and understands that "forward and round" are not mutually exclusive but parts of the totality of his movement.

Wednesday, September 17, Lesson 14

Did I mention patience? Did I mention patience both with the horse and with myself? It is not the horse's responsibility to initiate patience; it is mine to have it toward him and toward myself. This is a time in the training where there are no large, glorious breakthroughs and my mind is anxious for change. This is where control comes in. Shaman is doing as I ask, just not "tuned" enough. The walk is still hesitant though we have enlarged his space. The trot is still difficult and the few steps offered are followed by a quick return to the walk. The transition from halt to walk is still sluggish and not prompt.

Now I am deliberately going to turn the tables and take stock of everything that is in place. Shaman is very good at the "give" response and yields in the jaw and at the poll, softly moving the bit in his mouth all the while. He is getting quite accomplished at yielding both shoulders and hips in the work in-hand and does a creditable shoulder-in to the right, a progressively loosening and larger one to the left. He is very proud of his ability to "whoa" and stands stock still waiting for praise. His rhythm in the trot on the lunge is excellent which indicates that his balance is improving and he is comfortable with "forward and round." Even his canter on the lunge is slow and lofty with just a tinge of excitement.

So just what is the problem? My expectations and only mine. Once again I am faced with the reality of the horse: he can do what he can do at any given time, no more no less. I am expecting that he can move freely into the trot under saddle by now, not taking into account his age and experience, just his good nature and willingness. I must remember that if the young horse is overfaced, confused, or frightened, all is lost. And with the horse, restoring his trust once it is lost may never be possible.

And so we will continue to play and reassure Shaman that he is a "good boy" and any effort from him is greatly appreciated.

Saturday, September 20, Lesson 15

The resistance to go into the trot has now manifested itself in another way. When I began to tighten the girth today, Shaman cow-kicked with his left hind and was promptly rewarded with a smack on his flank. It didn't occur to me then but I remember now some history of kicking the farrier and the owner warning me about his left hind. Today Shaman spread his cards on the table.

The initial lungeing and work in-hand went well but under saddle the work proved to be a challenge. When I asked Shaman to move out of the halt and into the walk, he cow-kicked at my leg aid with his left hind. This was repeated several times until it escalated to two full-fledged bucks at the halt. I dismounted and put him back on the lunge. Forward was the immediate goal and forward he went, falling once but recovering and proceeding to a second work in-hand session. The goal in the work in-hand was again forward but always with the whip touching his side for the "and, walk-on" transition in an attempt to desensitize him slightly to the leg aid under saddle. I remounted, he stood quietly at the halt, we walked on a few steps with no incident, halted again, and we ended the session. The war was not won but the battle was, at least in part.

Monday, September 22, Lesson 16

Retracing the steps along the way can sometimes lead to a useful if not profound conclusion about the nature of the animal in question and how to proceed. The need for perfection when dealing with the horse is not so much a lofty ideal as it is an attention to each detail of his schooling so that nothing is overlooked. The retracing is the act of seeing exactly where the resistance occurs, meeting it there, and creating the perfect response from the horse.

Today when tightening the girth there was no cow-kick but Shaman's left hind was cocked defensively. Make a note: this is his individual expression of unwillingness and will appear in some way in all facets of his schooling. Now, it is the target of my attack.

The lungeing was excellent today, very round and cadenced though the down transitions to halt were not as prompt and were a little ragged. (Could he actually be learning "forward" and trot is now more present in his mind than "halt?") Whatever the case, this lesson, as all others, would concentrate on "stop" and "go," the building blocks that have to be in place before anything new is tackled. This encompasses both the large concepts and the details making up those concepts wherein each small increment contributes to and reinforces the larger concept, in this case, "stop" and "go."

Work in-hand is the most excellent way of explaining to a horse exactly what is required of him without the distraction of a mounted rider and a new balance for him. Today we worked back and forth between the work in-hand and mounting and standing at the halt. Several defensive gestures on Shaman's part led me to proceed in this way: backing away from contact with the bit, stretching his head and neck upward, and the cocked left hind. All of these are manifestations of not wanting to be between my hands and legs and so we proceeded to work both ends toward the middle, which is where the horse should be.

I noticed today that as I prepared to mount, Shaman would cock his left hind and so I deliberately rebalanced him in-hand each time before I mounted so he was standing evenly on all four feet. After repeating this several times, I concentrated on keeping him round and in the bridle in-hand at the halt and eventually got it at the halt under saddle.

"Taking care of business" is the mantra now and nothing will escape.

Tuesday, September 23, Lesson 17

Softening a little since the last session, (at least toward the horse if not toward the work itself), proved to be a good thing. I always tell students that they can only go as quickly as the horse will allow so that is the way I will proceed with Shaman. The difference here however, is that we are not considering whether or not to advance a horse up through the levels or add a new "trick" to his repertoire, but to understand and reliably perform the basics of "stop and go" without complaint or confusion. Today we made more headway, not quite to where we were before in terms of distance or duration, but in terms of the horse's comprehension. In other words, he is learning, not merely being conditioned.

Since I had pretty much decided to focus on that left hind foot as a barometer of Shaman's thinking, I was particularly aware of his reaction to tightening the girth. There was none so no need for correction. I spent extra time walking to the head and asking him to lower it in relaxation which he did without hesitation.

The lungeing and work in-hand went well, (the halts on the lunge were back in place), so we proceeded directly to the "on/off" part of the lesson. I have found this way of working to be particularly valuable with some horses: those who are shy and have no confidence, those who are afraid of someone above them, those with lack of balance, and those who are apt to shy at anything new. In Shaman's case, he fits into another category altogether: those who test the person as they would another horse in the pasture for a higher position in the pecking order. He is still not quite sure of who is making the decisions but his efforts at questioning authority are half-hearted today. He is allowing himself to be "under" in the hierarchy. Time, repetition, consistency, and determination are my allies here.

And so we proceed. In the "on/off" work at the mounting block I dismounted three times when I felt the left hind cock and threaten. Rebalancing Shaman to stand squarely while being mounted cannot be done from the saddle at this point since he does not know the leg aids. Instead, I link it with the work in-hand where he does stand squarely. In the saddle after the third rebalancing we were ready to concentrate on contact with the bit. Since I already knew that my legs coming on his sides previously elicited "lock up" and buck from him, I kept them slightly away from his sides and again concentrated on the head. So far so good. When he became round in front he stepped back but without incident. It was time for the legs to come closer to his sides. He was listening so my next decision (quickly made) was to get a few steps forward but not with the usual means of request. I did not cluck, say "walk on," close my legs, or use the whip but instead, substituted something else in place of the original means of request: neck and head flexions. I flexed slowly left, right, left, right, and Shaman walked on. He went half a ten meter circle and halted of his own accord. I then asked with the voice for him to "walk on" and he complied with no resistance. This time I asked for the halt, more with my non-moving body than anything else, he again complied, and amid much praise, we ended the lesson.

It probably should be clarified here that the reason the neck and head flexions succeeded is twofold. First, they were not linked in Shaman's mind to anything he had previously formed a resistance to such as legs or whip, and second, done in a particular manner, they can purposely unbalance the horse in which case he has to take a step. Deliberately disengaging the horse can also be looked at as unlocking or freeing him so he can proceed in movement.

Thursday, September 25, Lesson 18
    ...and here is how the horse's brain works: it works through association. Shaman is beginning to learn the formula:

On the bit = walk on.

He is learning it from the front first, but given the quick circulatory play of the aids, he has begun to figure out that round means forward. It is not difficult to associate the two. Today under saddle, as soon as he was put on the bit at the halt, he read my mind and walked forward with no hesitation. I lightly used my legs when he began to walk so that association could again be put in place and there was no resistance. I am pleased with his progress in the conceptual department and know that once the foundation is in place in each detail, there will be no problem with what at first glance seems elementary: halt-walk-trot-walk-halt. It seems fruitless, however, to teach these first without the quality in place. There is too much room for misunderstanding and chance occurrence and genuine communication is lost. Shaman's gift to me was this reaffirmation of complete adherence to the basics with no going ahead until they are understood calmly, quietly, and with no inkling of resistance from the horse. This is where the horse's mental balance is.

So we have a rather long paragraph extolling the virtues of uncompromising basics, (quality, if you will), but how about the left hind? Nothing showed up until the "on/off" mounting block work and then I had to rebalance him only once. He stayed square as I sat in the saddle so we went on to making him round and then to the walk.

Something should be said here about the attraction horses have for gates. The horse already knows that sidling toward the gate might just be the way to get to a more pleasant place, one in which he has food, buddies, and security. The attraction can be intense and overwhelming for the horse so rather than confront it when I may have the chance of losing the battle, I put something else in its place which requires the horse to place his attention back on me. Today when Shaman walked on under saddle, he went toward the gate. Knowing ahead of time that what he was doing was partially good but could quickly precipitate to something not good, I chose to halt away from the gate and reinforce his willing behavior by praising, dismounting, and repositioning him at the mounting block. When he walked on this time he flashed me the inkling of a picture which read: "straight – gate" so I immediately turned him to the right off the wall and we proceeded in a circle.

Perhaps the promise of the gate at this time initiated his forward movement in which case it worked in my favor but to let it control the further learning of the horse would not have been wise. Sometimes the natural environment can be used to a trainer's advantage but to rely on circumstance would only prolong the time between the lesson and the horse learning and making it his own. For any lesson given to the horse, the trainer is the horse's environment. There should be no other.

Friday, September 26, Lesson 19

…and speaking of the environment, today was absolutely one of the most wretched for schooling outside. It was in the forties, damp, windy, and the footing was sloppy, oozing mud. Even at a walk, Shaman's front feet slid forward several inches and the trot on the lunge was hard to keep going to the left. By the time we reversed, however, he had acclimated and relaxed his back and though not exactly swinging, it was not humped up and rigid.

The work in-hand was perfect in terms of how it is now being used. We have momentarily dispensed with the sideways steps in favor of skills that can immediately transfer and are needed for the under saddle work. Those skills are: walk on, immobile halt on all four feet, come onto the bit, small circles right and left, and short, straight lines.

Today should be titled, "Slow, but Forward." Even on the unsure footing, Shaman went forward at the walk with less hesitation and for longer periods. I began to move my legs more onto his sides, especially once he was in the walk. All in all, Shaman was more compliant and though he did drop his left hind at the halt, we walked through it and of course, it disappeared.

So just why would a basically good-natured guy like Shaman display the need to defend himself in such a manner? It's not really such a mystery if herd dynamics are considered, and the survival instincts they elicit from their members are understood. Each horse realizes he occupies his own space and his survival depends on it. When his space is invaded, all his cellular knowledge tells him to defend his space so that he can go on living; nothing less. The farrier picking up a leg deprives him of his balance on all four legs so his safety is compromised. Tightening the girth constricts his body so he is not ready for instant flight away from danger. Asking him for the "head down" position robs him of his ability to see that mountain lion lurking on the horizon. And finally, me mounting and asking him to carry me unbalances him and further corrupts his security when I insist that he be "on the bit." I have invaded his space and not only have I had the audacity to invade it, but now I am telling him just how he should position his body, when he should move and not move, and to remain calm through it all. Just who do I think I am?

The good natured guy is still there however, and it's my primary responsibility to keep his good nature and encourage it. I am, after all, expecting him to give up all his defenses and rely totally on me. That is, however, what he has already gone through in his own society. He will be dominated but the trade-off is, he will also be protected. This is the way it works in the herd. Let the trainer never forget it.

Sunday, September 28, Lesson 20

Today was Shaman's last lesson for a while. He will be brought out in the spring to continue his training.

We have arrived at a point where the foundation has been put in place. The foundation, however, has to be pliable enough to accommodate where the horse is at any given moment. There are quick trade-offs and quick reinstitutions of what is rewarded and what is overlooked in favor of a bigger concept. For example, when I ask the horse to "walk on" under saddle and he does so but stops after 6-8 steps, it is still acceptable since he did what I asked initially: he walked on from a halt. Staying in the walk until told to change is yet another concept that needs to be put in place: the maintaining of what is asked. In the horse's mind, it is an entirely different notion than the initial request. This is the one we are working on. When I feel he is going to come to a halt from the walk, I am just now able to push him on so he continues in the walk. The trick here is to ask for the halt before he decides to do it himself. It is a constant play of "his game/my game" with the intensity of a chess match. By the way, the breakdown of the initial response and the maintaining of that response is the same for the "on the bit" request. The initial giving to the bit is one thing; the maintaining of the give through movement and transitions is quite another. It is the maintaining that we are working on at this point, trying to prolong the response through time.

Since "forward and round" is the desired goal with any horse at any level, a few comments about teaching it to the young horse are in order.

To the horse, these concepts are in complete opposition. When he goes forward, he naturally lifts his head and neck and pushes his nose in front of the vertical, thus inverting his body. When the horse is round, however, he is resting or eating with his topline stretched and his head and neck down and toward the ground. The difficulty arises when you ask for both to be in place at once. Not that you ask for both simultaneously with the aids, (the aids are separated, albeit in lightning fashion), but the "go forward, be round" aids are so close to one another in time that the horse begins to associate one with the other. When an older horse with more schooling feels the legs come on, he should immediately come into the *ramener* position without the use of reins, flexing in the jaw and at the poll. With the younger horse, however, his association is the reverse. When he is put "on the bit" at the halt, he will walk on, and so it is with Shaman. He is beginning to understand that "forward and round" are aspects of the totality, not separate and distinct requests. Forward is round; round is forward. The message is: "I would like movement and I would like it in this fashion." It is a logical order that deals with the progression of energy, produced in the hindquarters and filtered and modified in the forequarters. It is a circulatory system, one which necessitates the aids being circulatory in nature also. In each stride, (in the case of the canter), or half stride, (in the case of the walk or trot), the trainer has the same message for the horse: "go forward, be round." Neither set of aids is prolonged, however. Each acts quickly followed by a complete relaxation of them. On the other hand, there is almost no time the trainer is not touching the horse, however briefly, with one or the other hand or leg. When one set of aids is active, the other is passive (receptive). In this way, the trainer both gets and gives information.

And so, where Shaman is now is where he will be when he comes back in the spring. He might be a little more reactive to outside stimuli but within a short reintroduction including lungeing and work in-hand, he should be quickly refreshed. Reminding usually has immediate results; teaching and instilling the concepts takes consistent and constant repetition.

Conclusion

No one can think or act as quickly as a horse which is why there is an element of artificiality going on when attempting to put on paper what can only be experienced. Construction of the sentence, the paragraph, the book, comes slowly. Making the horse, on the other hand, comes in quick but constant moments, each dependent on the last and each leading to the next. Like music, it is a creation and a practice of immediacy. And like music, it is never ending, dependent on foundation but ultimately reaching far above it.

And so, dear Shaman, think about what has occurred, sing your own song for now, but know that the duet is the measure of understanding between two voices and forms something much bigger than either one of us individually.

See you in spring.

The Mentor

Karl Bergmann, 1937 – 2008

In the beginning, he often told me: "You think too much." Coming from a teacher, this was somewhat of a surprise for me. After all, wasn't the object of the teacher to get the student to think? Not for Karl. His goal was rather, to erase all notions of right and wrong, all hierarchal positioning, in short, all preconceptions, so that the student could begin to experience. In a way, Karl wanted an empty mind in the student so that the horse could enter and begin to teach. No doubt he had seen far too many stifled riders who got nowhere because their minds were stuffed with information.

And so, his lessons seemed endless. (It takes time, after all, for the mind to go blank!) Over and over, the same track, the same tempo, the dulling effect of repetition for its own sake, and all without comment. Clearly the lesson I was taking was not like anything I had imagined beforehand. Where were the words? The instructions? The explanations? I felt like Sisyphus, condemned to push the same pebble up the same mountain, only to have it roll back down again. And on into the eternity of the arena track I went, round and round, until I was numb.

It wasn't until many years later that I understood. No, it wasn't the absolute obedience that Karl wanted in the student. It was indeed the blank mind. He, more than anyone, had fully realized the "necessity of doing," and that it was a kind of super-reality to the human, only everyday to the horse. He understood that to be fully aware of the horse, the rider had to shut out the critical and the contemplative and just keep going. In this was peace; in this was stillness. In this was harmony between horse and human. "Just keep going" – like the horse.

After months of going large and changing direction only across the diagonal, the arena sported foot high banks on the walls and appeared strangely pristine in its interior; no hoof prints, no uneven marks of travel, like my brain, it had gone blank. It did not register any deviation or indeed, any confirmed path except around its perimeter. It was then that I heard the words: "Down center line."

I was startled into indecision. What center line? When? From this short side or the next? Should I plan for a halt at "X?" And at what gait do I continue?

Bravely, I made a decision and on the far wall, turned right down center line. Predictably I overshot the letter and had to correct for it. No further directions came so I continued over "X" at the trot and glanced up ahead of me to see – Heaven help me –Karl rooted exactly at "C." I listened for directions but no words came. Karl was looming ever larger so I quickly made the decision to track left at Karl. I had done the right thing, I just knew it. I had changed direction using the center line. And then I heard it.

"Don't assume," came the gruff voice in a slow, measured assault.

I knew instantly that I had made the wrong choice. Instant confusion and self doubt. What else could I have done? I would have run him down if I had waited for his instruction. How could it have been wrong?

The flood of thoughts down the long wall consisted of recall, bewilderment, prediction, more bewilderment, and then: "Down center line."

Again I was put to the test, but what test? My dear horse obediently turned left and trotted down center line with adequate straightness but something had changed. This time I was aiming for "C." There was no one there, just the letter and the bend of the turn and then again the bend through the corner and then the lovely ironing out in straightness down the long wall, still on the left rein.

How did I get there? I don't remember a choice or an instruction or a voice. Ah, there it was: "Jawohl!" That one I knew. It meant the lesson was over.

Again the epiphany came much later. Once I had eliminated the preconceptions, I was able to ride the horse rather than the arena. I had come to understand that the right course of action was not always what it seemed to be. Many times it took a "turn" in quite an opposite direction altogether and it was this realization that freed me.

So in a sense, Karl's first lesson taught "doing" and that eternity of repetition.

His second allowed "being:" that depth of existence in which the doing had been mastered and relegated to its place as mere acquisition of skill. Once I did not assume and try to calculate the course, the course was there, rolling along with me. There was no separation in time or place, just stillness in movement. My horse and I came from a single thought, a single impulse, wherever we were at whatever time. All else had disappeared – even Karl.

And there it was again, the arena smoothed and dampened by a welcome mid-summer rain. Nothing tires like dust and today there would be none. I was refreshed simply by the thought. Newly dragged or newly moistened, the arena was always a forgiving surface. It inspired.

We had some time ago begun to carve up the large rectangle into a bounty of geometric shapes. This particular morning we began our session on the twenty meter circle at "A," making frequent transitions in direction and between gaits. This went on for twenty minutes or so with Karl frequently glancing down at his wristwatch. I was lulled by the steady rhythm with no expectancy of change and then it came: "Go large."

Since we were already tracking left on the circle, at "A" we continued down the short wall and into the first corner. The previous circle had made my horse supple, bringing him to my aids, so the first corner was simply a continuation into what had been well prepared. Memory of the bend comes along with straightening and makes it possible for the horse to be four-square underneath and so the long wall proved effortless. We went into the next corner, momentarily straight with my horse more underneath himself and then – oh, oh – a large puddle of water in the next corner. We'll just cut the corner short, avoid the mud, and resume on the next long wall, or so I quickly thought.

Somewhere after my little detour a wall of sound rose up. "Halt!" It could have stopped a tank.

"What are you doing?" came the angry words.

"You know, you're no good. Get off. Give the horse a break!" I was devastated.

"The horse doesn't care. You're the one who wouldn't go into the corner, not the horse."

While hosing off my horse back at the barn, there was no discussion, no explanation. All was duty in silence and then, "Tomorrow." As I heard the sound of Karl's tires on the gravel driveway, I noticed I was standing in a puddle.

There would prove to be many tomorrows before this lesson came back to me in all its potency. At the time, I was humiliated, yes. But even the feeling of utter worthlessness mercifully wore off through the passage of time while the intense memory remained.

Through the years there would be many occasions with a horse where I would act out of convenience rather than what the horse needed at the moment. The puddle in the arena corner was just such an incident. I could almost hear Karl say, "Don't project!" Again, he called me back to the horse.

One of the most unproductive ways in which the human deals with the horse is to force his views and feelings onto the poor animal. This also smacks of extreme arrogance since we thereby deny the horse his own particular way of being and hence, his existence. But it is common. After all, wasn't the horse created to serve us? Are we not innately superior which accords us full license to do with him as we see fit?

Not exactly for Karl. He was not only a realist but a super-realist. For him, the horse would show you he understood only after you mastered his language. It was not enough to put your heels down and keep your hands quiet. In other words, you had to not only do what the horse needed, you had to become who the horse needed. In this alone, Karl made the leap from trainer of the horse to teacher of the human. He was, in essence, demonstrating what he had gone through, what his life had been about. He was transferring the greatest gift he had: his own existence. It would remain up to me as the student to take it and make good use of it.

Remembering Karl is not difficult. He is as much a part of me as my own inescapable genetic make-up. His words, (which he never thought I would hear) – "She's good but don't tell her" – continue to half-halt, but send me forward. He knew that the worth of a life was in the passing through it. And that is what he has done. And, so admirably.

Rest well, my friend. And watch well. As you have taught.

The Way is Dressage

Table of Contents

	Preface	147
Chapter 1	What is Art?	148
Chapter 2	The Basics	152
Chapter 3	On the Bit	157
Chapter 4	Dressage as Metaphor	161
Chapter 5	Zap	163
Chapter 6	Dom	174
Chapter 7	The Aid Formula	176
Chapter 8	The Mêlée	180
Chapter 9	Paradoxical Dressage	184
Chapter 10	The Language of Live	187
Chapter 11	The Three Ts	193
	About the Author	199

Preface

As the trainer advances on her journey, the distance from her subject decreases. If she completes said journey there will be no distance at all. Two of the essays in this book are meant to illustrate this idea: "Zap" and "The Three T's." They are both written in first-creature, not first person, so not only has the trainer disappeared; the author may have also!

So welcome to dressage not as practice but as a "way." And what is that way, you ask? That will be your journey, my friend. May it be your most rewarding.

—Susan Medenica, 2014

What is Art?

How extraordinary that this could even occur! That one could take a four-legged creature out of the open spaces, place him underneath a two-legged creature of enclosure, and produce a work of art! Just how do these necessary, contrary states combine and agree to produce an image unlike any other in existence? One in which precisely because of extreme difference, extreme cohesion emerges?

The answer is: art.

In art, all is possible and yet "art" often results in a mishmash of arbitrary ingredients that neither complement each other nor combine to form something greater. They remain isolated possibilities, and so it is most often with the horse and the human. Each remains alone, apart, in vitality and good intent but, they wait. Nothing is changed, nothing is greater, nothing is worthy of attention until – the foundation and the vision spark into agreement. Like the original big bang theory of the creation of the universe, the collision of one particle with another jumps into new life and thus new possibility is born. In this case, that new possibility is the art of dressage.

Dressage is a collaborative art. Much like music and dance, it is created from the input of more than one creature and is the only art in which a non-human participates in its creation. This makes it truly unique for to include an animal in this hallowed human endeavor is not easily accepted. Art is the domain of the human, or so goes accepted thinking.

And yet, "possibility" within human conception is limitless. It is what takes us above the mundane concerns of the day and elevates us to a position of unabashed truth. We are rendered speechless. In which other art do two creatures meet, disappear as individuals, and reappear as an entirely new entity? And it is no mere coincidence that it is the horse with whom we collaborate.

The horse, more than any other creature on earth, is the creature who inspires. He is history itself. He is the inhabitant of myth, legend, and dream. By virtue of his particular qualities, we escape, we conquer, we rise above. We are greater with than without him and it is for this reason that the art of dressage is born. It takes us to a place we alone cannot enter. But then, neither can the horse.

As much as this collaboration defies definition, so does art. As such, they are the perfect match. Neither can be boiled down to absolutes, graded for accuracy, analyzed for content, harnessed to plow the field. For dressage to be art, mystery must be present and it is precisely this quality that hooks us. It's the "Wow" factor. We know it when we see it but we cannot define it. It nevertheless speaks to us like nothing else. It gets to us "where we live," as they say. So how do we even begin to talk about this phenomenon?

While art may defy definition, it does present us with certain characteristics. These are not so much laws as they are qualities aiming at something "other than." Suffice it to say that with art, if we can name it easily, it probably is not art.

When we are fortunate enough to be in the presence of a work of art, the first thing that should strike us is craft. The image or the sound should emerge with an utter ease of delivery springing from an unsurpassed technique. There should be no question in the mind of the viewer or listener as to what if? Will it? Can it possibly? The viewer is immediately assured that the work will not crumble due to lapses in craft. All has been seen to. This is, after all, the foundation on which the idea depends. It must be in place.

Craft is the most measurable of all the characteristics of a work of art. It is the easiest to verbalize about and such is the case with competitive dressage. Each performance is judged and rated according to a preordained set of movements and each of these movements must begin and end at a prescribed place in the arena. This is the score-keeping aspect of technique and belongs in the arena of sport. It is a tally, nothing more.

In the art of dressage, however, it is precisely the craft that disappears. On some level we know it is there and it must be, but when perfected, it vanishes in favor of the more profound. The enactment has become so simple for both horse and rider that they are on to new realms of expression. Their unsurpassed mastery of the physical is taking them there.

When we leave the physical, there has to be more. If there is not, we are dealing with sport. If there is, we are in the realm of art and even though the following concepts dwell in the metaphysical, it is still possible to describe toward definition, the characteristics that are present. (Perhaps this is the art of art?)

After craft, the mechanics, if you will, there must be something more. There has to be meaning. In other words, a work of art has to possess and give rise to something more than what it is at face value. Meaning is a measure of its content.

In the art of dressage, the horse and human collaborate in the process of creation. There is no other art in which this happens. While it is true that humans and animals form partnerships for sundry reasons – work, play, companionship – this is the only instance in which the goal is art. And, this alone places dressage in a unique position among the other arts.

Closely linked to the meaning inherent in a work of art is what motivates that meaning to become reality: vision. Vision is what lifts us from the ordinary, everyday concerns of life and sets us afloat in a world of endless possibility. And it is the horse who inspires us to transcend.

For dressage to be art, both the vision of the human and that of the horse must be present. As much as the horse is influenced by the human, it has to turn reciprocal: the human must also be influenced by the horse. This is the allowance where each absorbs the essence of the other and makes it his own so that the horse becomes more human and most importantly, the human more horse. It is the art of empathy and from this movement into the other, new inspiration is discovered.

The final two characteristics are linked within the space/time continuum. Both universality and timelessness are expansive notions, ones without which, however, the definition of art would not be possible.

Universality needs no translation. It is equally applicable to all species and within ours. There are no schisms or misunderstandings since universality demands pertinence to all. In this sense, it is the language of "live." Comprehended by all.

Universality is at the core of being. It is what each of us has in common with the other, the pulse of all life beating for the same reason. When it is expressed through art, it strikes us immediately and we are given pause, speechless yet rapt; and so it is when dressage enters this arena. The horse and human are expressing nothing less than that elusive yet fundamental possibility that from the unique outlook of each, commonality is born. The horse and human have become so cohesive that ones breath becomes the other's, unified in purpose. Such a picture speaks to all. A sigh escapes.

Part of the indestructibility of a work of art is in its timelessness, our final characteristic. It does not pander to current fads, harken back to the "good old days," or predict the next revolution. Its relevance does not depend on timeliness. Instead, a work of art crashes through that boundary of measurement and frees us immediately and for ever after.

To accomplish this, however, dressage does exist in three dimensions simultaneously. In this way it connects us to all that is embedded in the past yet pioneers us into the future. And it is this magic of vision over foundation, occurring in the ever-present, that is so captivating in the performance of dressage. When the horse and human enter the arena they at one and the same time represent the sincere past from which they take the inspiration and the discipline, and the obsession with the future, which is filled with need and constancy. And it is only within this special union where it comes to pass since the horse carries all forever in the present. Step by step, stride by stride, they pass but stay in the glow of the art.

A work of art is indisputable. While "classical" may express craft and harmony, (book one), and "dressage" may express beauty and unity, (book two), "art" is in a completely different realm. It does not operate or behave in traditional ways. It defies analysis. Its constituent qualities are so firmly woven together that whichever one attempts to single out immediately become something else. And this is the "way" it happens.

So let it go, let it be. Let it rise to fruition, let is rise to existence.

The Basics

The horse must be available to the trainer and for this to happen, certain fundamental concepts must be in place. These have little to do with the common practice of advancing through the levels via patterns and the "training scale." Instead, these concepts present to the horse the vocabulary he is to learn and take with him throughout his life. They also reassure him that his trainer knows and is fluent in this language so that misunderstandings are limited and of short duration. Once these concepts are learned, the horse will have little difficulty performing the movements of the high school with complete precision and expression. In short, he will be educated.

Contrary to accepted practices in the training of the horse, the concepts presented here should be taught simultaneously, not one after the other. One is not of greater importance than the next but each addresses one facet within the horse that must not be left untouched until a further time. There is no "climbing the ladder" here. We are working horizontally, taking what the horse gives us and responding immediately by correcting or sanctioning. In other words, we are treating the whole horse from the onset as we want him to be when finished. We are not going to practice wrong; we are going right for perfection in all our dealings with the horse.

The Give

Of all the ideas presented to the horse, the most important is, and always will be, the "give." It is not only square one in simply being with the horse but also permeates his entire training and is prerequisite for the delicate and precise movements of the haute école. A complete lack of resistance from the horse is the goal, involving not only his entire body but his mind as well. He should not resist with any particle of his being.

If we examine the mechanics of the herd, we will see over and over again that the horse who moves another horse is the leader. In essence, what the leader is doing is to get his subordinate to give and in this case, the "lower" horse cedes his space. Though we may not agree with his government, the society of the horse is a hierarchal one and as such, accepts a leader. There is no room for dissention and for the horse to show his acquiescence, he gives. This ensures stability for all since the receptive horse can now be directed to greener grass, away from a predator, and back to the safety of the herd.

In practical terms, what this means is that whatever we ask the horse to do, he does without question. This of course presupposes we know precisely how to ask and even more importantly, what to expect as a response and how to answer that response.

What are we doing when we want the horse to have his feet trimmed? We are systematically asking him to "give" each foot in turn. It sounds simple but for the horse, it requires that he: remain immobile, rebalance in four different positions on only three legs, and over-flex his joints. Even this rudimentary requirement begins to look complex but we have a lot further to go; our dressage horse is only on the welcome mat!

"Give" is fundamental to dressage. It is all we ever ask but we ask it in countless ways and for countless purposes. From the softening of the jaw, to the yielding of the rib cage, the horse learns to move away from pressure, to be caught by it, to be shaped by it, and finally, to stay within its boundaries by the mere suggestion of it. The well-rehearsed "give" has now evolved into the given in that the horse has agreed to be where and in what manner we wish him to be. And, he is there precisely through lack of resistance.

Stop and Go

The ability of the horse to give to pressure leads directly to the next basic: stop and go. This fundamental idea is often given short shrift in the mind of the trainer but it is primary in getting the horse with his trainer. If the horse does not heed this directive, the training cannot proceed for this very basic choice is at the core of who the horse is: a prey animal. What this means for us is that he is at all times ready to fly away from perceived danger. He is immobile only when he is secure which is why this directive is of such importance. It is the measure of how he feels about his trainer.

As a prey animal, the horse is instructed by his instinct. This is what he will obey if nothing else is in place. He is supremely aware of his environment and it is for this reason that the stop-go message is so important. It proves that his instinctive reaction has been supplanted by our instruction. It further proves that trust has become more influential than instinct. And it is only by achieving this status with the horse that the education can proceed. When the horse is perfectly balanced at the halt and shows absolutely no indication of movement, it is a simple matter to ask him to move. By a decontraction of the aids, the horse will move. A little aside here – it is not through tension in the aids that the horse moves; it is by relaxation. Tension in the aids will contract and eventually stop the horse because it stops the movement of energy from back to front moving through the horse.

Go left/Go Right

The next focus should be on the horse moving left and moving right. With each animal there will be a difference in the sides but it is not as simple as stiff or hollow. Individual parts of the horse's body make up the differences and it should be in these locations of resistance that we work for the sake of flow within the whole horse.

When resistance appears, it should be met immediately with like resistance of a slightly greater degree in order to illicit a softening from the horse. This very act of transforming resistance to yielding, (the "give"), is the most important response we will ever receive from our horse since it is what opens him up for the free flow of energy that we need access to; it is our modeling clay, if you will.

What we are seeking from the horse is a greater degree of ambidexterity than we ourselves possess. There will never be complete equality from side to side however. One side will never appear or function as the other but each will grow in strength and suppleness as they are addressed singly.

As in countless other instances in life, there are trade-offs and this is not less so when considering sidedness in the horse. As a rule, the horse moving left will be stronger, slower, and will display more amplitude in his stride. While these qualities are desirable, what accompanies them is less so. Because the horse is stronger in himself, he will "confront" your aids in this manner also, making it difficult to attain the soft acquiescence of the cultivated animal.

On the flip side, when going right the horse will be more supple and hence more compliant, his gaits will have less scope, and he will tend to duck behind the aids. He will also display his natural predilection for going left by counter flexing his head and neck to the left, bulging his rib cage to the right, and edging his haunches to the right. It is usually on this side that straightness is a problem.

Bend to Straight

To help eliminate the natural sidedness in our horse, the next concentration should be on bending to straightening. This is the ideal exercise and probably the most important transition the horse will ever make because it cannot help but to involve his entire body as well as his acceptance of and ability to change.

When done well, bending to straightening is proof of balance between suppleness and strength. One without the other will never make the horse totally available to us. In other words, he will naturally display a crooked straightness and an uneven bend. But the ability to do both proves that multiple resistances have been addressed and eliminated.

Bending to straightening is all about how energy flows within containment: bending increases, straightening unleashes. Bending brings the horse together in softness because the line directly from hind to fore is curved. This allows for a judicious shaping of the horse as he straightens, reminding him that his power can proceed in lightness. And with these two qualities in place, collection is a given.

Here again, we are working with seeming opposites within the horse that must come together in common purpose, each acting on the other to modify. The goal is strength in lightness. The way to it is bend to straight.

Forward/Round

In a sense, "go forward, be round" exemplifies and is proof of all other directives being in place. It is the summation, if you will, of all we ever want from our horse. If he understands "give," he can be made round. If he understands "stop and go," he is, of course, forward. Once the horse can go left and go right, he is displaying a different kind of roundness: that throughout the length of his body. And of course "bend to straight" enhances this but also demands that the horse stay round while he is making this transition and moving forward.

The message "go forward/be round" says to the horse: "move, but in this way." It is not enough to move without shape and it is not enough to be inertly round. (Even the immobile halt should be full of energy!) Both must come together, quickly and precisely, each modifying the other, until it is understood by the horse that there is no forward without round nor round without the energy of forward. They are inexorably linked.

Much like the potter at his wheel, the trainer is dealing with the constant passage of time and how it informs change. Unlike clay, however, the horse will constantly change of his own volition. While the message "go forward/be round" may be constantly the same, it has within it the ability to address any and all behaviors the horse offers, and that is its strength. When done with proper proportion of the aids, it will also elicit from the horse a kind of dance, full of ease and purpose. From it, all will be possible, all will be there for the asking.

Conclusion

To speak the language fluently and with precision should be the goal of any trainer. When addressing the horse, however, this is not so simple since the language we are speaking is native to him, not to us. The basics presented here are offered to bridge this gap between how the horse understands already, and how to present our messages like a native speaker so that conversation is possible. The one-sided conversation is only a speech. The two-way conversation, however, gives rise to what one alone cannot come up with: the expression of beauty incarnate.

On the Bit

Make no mistake about it. The term "on the bit" is the most misunderstood phrase in the last one hundred years of academic dressage. For some, it is the rigid, compressed headset; for others, it is the languishing head in alleged lightness. These positions would seem to define the outline, but they have nothing to do with the purpose of placing the horse "on the bit," namely: to put the horse in the best form for carrying the rider, to place the horse in his own position of relaxed balance, and last but certainly not least, to provide an unbroken conduit for communication between horse and human.

While it is true that each horse has his own particular relation with the bit, his personal signature, if you will, there are genuine distinctions between the horse who willingly adopts the bit as part of himself, and the horse to whom the bit is a gross assault on his being. Unfortunately, it is most often the latter that we witness and so it has become the accepted norm without so much as the raising of an eyebrow. But as we know, the truth has little to do with what we suppose and so it is with the "on the bit" position.

When the horse is "on the bit," he is just that: he is on top, he is over. He is not against, behind, or above. He is in a position both physically and mentally to move the bit himself thereby making it his own and by extension, an additional avenue for self-expression. This of course presupposes the rider's aim is to create through suggestion, not mandate.

In order for the horse to be able to achieve this attitude, the bit must be allowed to hang within the horse's mouth, not lay on it. And this is precisely the difference between lightness and traction, the quality of being alive or dead to the hand. And of course, this is exactly what leads to that much coveted state where the horse is in self-carriage or "en parole." But it is only achievable through a complete and unbiased understanding of the horse's relation to and perception of the bit. This is a crucial point of meeting between horse and human.

As with any direct statement, there must be the accompanying support to give it breadth and foundation. Validity is based on this support and so it is with the "on the bit' dilemma. The horse either is or is not on the bit and the proof must be evident one way or the other.

There are two ways in which we can judge whether or not the horse is on the bit: by vision and by sensation. On the ground we can of course see, but from the horse's back, we must feel. Both must be learned. The eye must know the correct shape; the body must know the correct feel. Perception and accuracy are key here. They must play back and forth as each confirms the other.

The Look

The first impression of a horse correctly on the bit is one of wholeness and integration within his entire body. There are no sharp angles or jutting limbs; only soft flow. The whole horse is presented as a convex arc, rising upwards from the haunches, to the shoulders, to the head, anchored on the earth but lifting into the air. What perfect negotiation between these two elements. Only the horse, and only the horse in this position could achieve such uncommon elegance.

When the horse is on the bit, his neck stretches in a perfect, unbroken arc made up of absolutely equal degrees with no flatness (not even one inch!) along the topline. The neck appears soft and yielding, not molded and fixed in an artificial frame. There is some undulation indicating the energy is flowing through, not dammed up. It is all about allowing movement, not curtailing it.

One of the most controversial aspects of being on the bit is how the head should look. While the theorists maintain that the nose should be "slightly" in front of the vertical, the picture most often seen now is of the head decidedly behind the vertical. Neither is correct. When the nose is in front of the vertical, the horse is pushing, thus dropping his back and attempting to invert his neck in small degrees. His jaw has not flexed enough to produce the uninterrupted arc of the topline and he is in a steady traction against the hand.

When the horse is behind the vertical, there is the danger that he may also be behind the bit, meaning he has disappeared from the contact altogether. While this is not always the case, it is an extreme and by encouraging this, the horse will soon learn he is only a hair's breadth away from not being able to be influenced because literally, he cannot be found.

When the horse is on the bit, however, his face line is exactly on the vertical; not ahead, not behind. The jaw has flexed to the degree that it allows the bit to hang in the mouth, not rest on it. This eliminates the too much or not enough contact problem: too much because the horse is being held; not enough because the conduit is not direct. And, the contact is interrupted.

The contact itself is evident in the reins which are the conduits between the horse and human, carrying the thoughts of both in turn. They are live, not static. When all is going well, there appears to be air in them as if there is breath pulsing through them. Though the lines are direct from hand to mouth there is a liveliness in their frequent undulations. This is what keeps the face on the vertical for it is the best position in which the horse can both receive and send thought.

And finally, the ears should be addressed. They are, after all, the indicators of where the horse's attention is. Ears forward are a no-no. The horse's attention is on anything but the rider and as might be expected, this is usually accompanied by a short, cramped neck, the face behind the vertical, and the rider with entirely too much in his hands. The horse and rider are at a stand-off with traction from each, substituting for balance and conversation between the two. When the horse is on the bit, totally focused on the rider, his ears go back and to the sides, often flopping in rhythm and relaxation with each stride. It is a telltale sign.

The Feel

While vision is an objective perception that can be measured, feel resides in a more nebulous realm and can therefore best be described. As in a work of art, the underlying structure is certainly there but it is the voice, the message, the subjective feel that carries the greatest impact: and so it is from the back of a horse.

By definition, "on the bit" is light, very light, but the feel is still there. Lightness is not nothingness, It is a presence in the hand, a kind of vital pulse between horse and human that carries the language. When lightness is missing, the horse and rider are in traction against each other and language is not possible. The two are at an impasse. When there is "air" in the reins, however, a gentle circular flow of exchange takes place with each creature allowing the other the time to savor.

In the fingers there will be a dovetail feel, always there but never mechanical. The true conversation takes time and – the response is always pertinent to what was just said. So as you end what you have to say to the horse, he begins. As he ends what he has to say in response, you begin. In this way the feel is uninterrupted but varies constantly in an unbroken wave. This is one speaking to the other and in this way, refinement takes place. You are both of the same wave, both contributing. You are both necessary, you are both fulfilled by the other.

The feel of the horse being "on the bit" is not limited to the sensations in the fingers, however. Miraculously enough, the whole of the horse has been centered so that you feel him not only through surface contact but through invisible lines also: your seat bones are his hind legs as you walk forward, your shoulders are his shoulders as you bend gently into a shoulder-in. In this position the horse's back has risen underneath so you have a place to sit but most importantly, the horse can now carry in comparative ease. Because the back has risen, the hind legs can come further under the mass of the horse and when they do, the shoulders rise. You are in a place of stillness, quiet and connected. There are only the constants of position and flow.

In addition to the bodily sensations given to the rider by the horse being on the bit, there is a feel imparted to the mind also: an immediate astonishment that such power under the seat could translate to such lightness in the hand. This is the essence of the ideal piaffe, a movement offered, not demanded. And when you receive, there are times when the hind legs will land in your hands, the heart will beat in your palms, and there are times when the breath moves softly in and out of your own body as you receive the gift.

And so the mind is amazed, the body grateful. This is nothing less than the manifestation of heaven on earth, the dream arising from the firm foundation, and we come to it via the particular position which gives rise to this possibility: the "on the bit" position.

Dressage as Metaphor

"What we're doing out there is not really what we're doing out there," she said, gesturing over her shoulder to the dressage arena behind her.

"We are not cruising letter to letter on an artificially manicured horse. We are not playing a game of win or lose. We are not achieving some pre-set goal of excellence nor are we striving for notoriety."

Here she removed her glasses and cleared her throat.

"What we're doing out there is the rehearsal of life itself, nothing less. And it is for this reason that we are given the horse. He is the other in whom we resonate or from whom we are repelled. He is the measure of our life now, and now, and now, and he is the measure of the quality of that life."

Again she paused.

"All else is illusion."

In its most basic sense, metaphor is comparison. However, it is not quite that simple. The reason for using metaphor is to say something easily apprehended while referring to something far deeper, far more complex, and far more eternally meaningful. It is a way to teaching. It is the act of acute perception. It is the invitation to dive deep.

And so the action that goes on in the dressage arena has more to it than mere game pieces moving around on a playing board. In fact, it might be said that dressage occurs outside its own mechanical movements and patterns, outside its own boundaries, if you will. One does not ride the movement to ride the movement. One rides the movement because that movement leads to something else: it makes the horse more beautiful in himself. In other words, one rides the horse, not the arena. In this sense, whatever one does is something more.

In the creation of dressage it is easy to see what level of awareness is being presented and this is totally the choice of the rider. Most will play the game and present superficially lustered horses obeying directives that are shortsighted and somewhat arbitrary. It is this standard that is so sought after and this is how measurement can be used to proclaim good/better/best. It is convenient and satisfying. But the truth lies further down and ultimately more inward than mere movement.

It is actually quite simple. When one looks at the picture being presented, one should ask, what is and what is not. The reality may be readily apprehensible but the truth lies far beneath the surface. As in the creation of music, there are the notes but it is how these notes are delivered that transcends the reality of the notes themselves. And it is precisely the same in dressage.

The reality is the movements the horse performs but the truth is the movement of the creature himself. It is this that tells us who he is and who he is with.

And of course this leads to the measure of a life: at one and the same time, what is its purpose individually and what is its value among others?

One of the unique possibilities within the practice of dressage is the opportunity it gives each of us to understand who we are as individuals by virtue of who we are with the horse. He is the supreme measure because he is just waiting for each of us to get it right. He, after all, already knows how to be a horse. His society is a model of flow toward the common good.

The same is not true of the human species, however. We are fond of playing the dangerous game of illusion wherein our actions arise from what we want, not from what we need. We claim reality but disregard truth. We are easily duped.

With the horse, this cannot be so. He does not acknowledge illusion. He simply looks the other way. And this is why he is the perfect measure of a vision of truth: he cannot be corrupted. And so when we place ourselves in conjunction with him, we, each of us has the possibility of knowing who we are at base. We are stripped of pretense, laid bare, and driven inward to our core. We have transcended not in the usual sense, by rising upward, but by traveling inward and here is the beauty of the move. We now discover our own self and in the process find that we are connected, interconnected, if you will, to this creature standing before us. I am me, he is him, but we take the same breath. We are in a state of permeation where we pass into the horse, affecting every part of him. He likewise has entered into us and we receive. By this we know: one life equals all life. There can be no other realization possible.

If this sounds like a journey, it is. If it sounds like a process, it is. If this describes growth, it most certainly is for it is in the doing, the growing, the change, that we become. And this has no end.

"So what is it we are doing out there?" She finally asked.
Silence.
"Precisely," she answered her own question.
"We are, each of us, becoming. As is the horse. It is the passing, it is the doing, it is the way."
Silence and then:
"*The way is dressage.*"

Zap

"My son," said the aged dappled stallion in a calm, wise voice. "Stop your antics and listen. I wish to talk to you about something you are going to experience very soon and something that will follow you throughout your life."

Here the young fireball gave a mighty kick with his hind legs and ears pricked forward, trotted up to his father.

"Ya, Dad," he said, eager to be off and running again. "What?" He stomped impatiently with his right front leg; spring was here.

"You are about to experience 'Zap.'" His father answered, giving the word in question a particularly percussive delivery. "And you will never forget it."

The young colt stomped impatiently once more. He was bored and eager to be on his way.

"'Zap' is a surprise at first; then you come to expect it," continued the father, "and…"

Here the sentence stopped short for the red colt had bolted off away from his father and toward a swarm of fluttering yellow butterflies. They looked like they were having a jolly time and the young one tried to join the wafting circle.

"Son," roared the old one. "Come here. Now!"

The butterflies were no fun anyway and dispersed as soon as junior tried to join their circle.

"Ya, ya, Dad," the young one answered back and again trotted over to his father albeit this time in resignation. He could tell something was up.

"My young man," the father began again. "You have no respect for knowledge and that will eventually get you into trouble. You act on urge, not on experience, but you will learn. Eventually."

Here the young man dropped his head and slowed his twitches except on the left flank where he was being tickled intermittently by something that kept returning. Tickle and twitch and twitch and tickle; it was spring.

Beginning with a deep sigh, the father continued. "As I was saying, you are about to learn what each horse in turn experiences throughout his life. You are about to meet 'Zap,' and it will affect you always."

Here the colt bent his head in closer to his father. Just maybe the old man had something to say. It wouldn't hurt to give it a shot. Now if only he could stop that persistent tickle. There it was again, twitch, twitch.

"'Zap' is quick but remorseless. It is there and gone in less than a blink, but its effect on you will be profound. You will never forget it. You will…"

Here the old one stopped short. With a loud, high neigh, the colt had taken off running, punctuating each stride with a powerful kick to the rear. He was frantic. His path was erratic; first one way, then the other. He had to get away and what he knew was to run. His head was low. He was unaware of all but the sting to his left flank.

"Watch out son!" The father bellowed, but it was too late. With his extreme concentration on getting away, our young friend had not seen the three horizontal lines in front of him. "Pow!" He reeled back momentarily and shot forward again.

"Here son. Here," the elder yelled but it was to no avail. The colt was in even more earnest to get away. The sky was indeed falling. There was nothing to do but run and kick and kick at the latest assailant. Now the flank was fine. It was the neck that inspired. Panic had come to life.

The aged stallion slowly shook his head several times. He was the epitome of the all-knowing one. He had experience, he had knowledge. Now if only…

"Come here, son," the old gentleman offered in a low voice. "It's over. Come here."

By now the frenzy had passed and the colt was just trotting in circles, periodically blowing loudly through his nose; an editorial comment.

"Son. Come here," the father repeated. "You are fine. It will be allright," he said soothingly.

The colt by now had dropped to a walk but his head was still reeling from his recent encounters and his body was wet. If only he had longer legs, he knew he could have gotten away, but away from what? He knew he was meant to run; all his herd-mates did it, even his father on occasion.

"And you thought running was only for play," the elder began slowly. "True, we run when we are happy, but we also run when we are scared. And this time you were scared. Twice, as I saw it."

The colt hung his head and neck and slowly approached his father. The electric tingles through his body had disappeared but he was worn out. All he could do was stand motionless, close to his father. He knew there were more words coming.

"My young fellow," the wise one began again. "I was trying in some way to prevent what just happened to you but alas, I was too late. Experience, not knowledge, had to be your teacher this time. Experience does turn into knowledge, however, but with some it takes time. I am here to shorten that time and to prepare you before you encounter something you can't handle."

Here the old grey cleared his throat slowly and deliberately. His son stood motionless; he was ready to listen.

"You have just encountered 'Zap,'" the lecture began. "The first was in the form of one of countless flying predators that besiege us in the warm months of the year. This one happened to be a bot fly and as is their habit, after he landed on you he entered your body with his sharp, pointed stinger. It only lasts a moment but its after-effects are frightening."

"But Father, why did this happen?" The colt inquired pitifully.

"That is anyone's guess. But it is part of reality and as such, we will meet it and we have to deal with it when we do. There is no other way."

"But then what happened?" It was the pathetic youth again.

"You ran into an electric fence," came the answer. "And electric is the essence of 'Zap.' It is a merciless force that strikes and withdraws before you even know it was there. It leaves you stunned but frantic. You run. And run some more as if running will save you. Ultimately, it won't. By running after the bot fly sting you ran right into the wires which stung you again. You had quite the experience today."

"Father. Is my whole life going to be like this?" The young fellow was despondent.

"Yes, and no." The father chuckled under his breath. It was time.

"What happened to you today was a wake-up call. You had the experience of 'Zap' – twice. Now it is time for you to turn that experience into knowledge. To simply react is not enough."

By now the red colt had started to dry and he was no longer twitching. But something had changed. In his new-found quiet, he was listening. He had never done this before; he hadn't had to. Everything had been fine until…just the faint remembrance sent a tremor throughout his small body.

"My son. Are you ready to listen now?" Began the father. "For there's more to the story."

"Oh, no," came the plaintive cry.

"Yes. There are two more 'Zaps' you will encounter as you pass through your life. And these are slightly different. They both come directly from the human."

"The what?"

"You remember the young girl who tried to approach you and offer you a treat? She is a human and the member of an entire species we call "humanoids." They are the ones who carry the next two 'Zaps.'"

The wise one saw that his son's eyes were beginning to close and that he was at last relaxed.

"But more of that later. You rest now. I'll be right here next to you."

The colt closed his eyes and slept. It was deep. He was working on what had just happened to him. Perhaps it was a way to knowledge?

165

"Welcome back, son," the grey one offered when he saw his son's eyes begin to open. "Did you rest well?"

"I th-th-think so," came the sleepy response followed by a large yawn.

"Good. You should be wide awake for what I am about to tell you. Let's take a little walk. I want to show you something."

And so the two proceeded slowly over to the section of their pasture that was closest to buildings, machinery, and the gate. It was a sunny, late spring day and the humanoids were slowly moving about, easing into the change of seasons with deliberate actions.

At a safe distance from the gate they halted. It was to be a peaceful lesson.

"Take a look at the gate, son. Do you see the long stick leaning up against it?"

The colt nodded slightly but barely saw what his father was talking about. He was beginning to feel restored and his attention was elsewhere, specifically on anything that moved: the trudging humanoids, the dog sniffing a fence post, and the butterflies. Ah, the butterflies. So happy. So carefree.

This time the colt did see, for a slight breeze had sprung up and the long lash of the whip was moving. It reminded him of a snake.

"That long stick is called a whip and it is often carried by humanoids. They believe it is a way of communicating with us but frankly, I have seen and felt it cause more confusion than anything else. Its possibilities for precision are not widely known."

"But what does it really do?" came the inquiry.

"I will tell you." The graceful elder cleared his throat and began.

"The whip is made up of two parts: the shaft and the lash. The lash is meant to make a loud crack in the air, or to sting our bodies when used directly on us. The first is the wake-up call; the second, the actual follow-through and yes, it does feel just like a fly bite or an electric fence."

A shudder of remembrance went through the colt.

"But Father, why would the humanoid wish to sting us?" (The young man was beginning to increase his vocabulary!)

"For any number of reasons: because we do not move when told to, because we do not move quickly enough, because the humanoid is a terribly busy creature and doesn't know what else to do so he flails his stick at us? It's my guess as well as yours. Most of the time the message is not clear."

The colt moved a few steps closer to get a better look at this mysterious instrument. It looked harmless enough just leaning up against the fence post. He tried to imagine the powers it might possess but couldn't. To him it looked just like a stick. Time to nibble on some grass anyway. It was spring and the green blades were long enough to pick.

Just then the young girl emerged and ran straight for the stick yelling, "out of there, out of there." She grabbed it and began running again, cracking the whip in mid-air as she went. "Out of there you chickens, you" she yelled as the lash snaked through the air. Once, twice, three times.

Both horses were by now at the far end of the pasture. It was as if the old one had known what was coming before the cracks were heard. He had taken off running with the young one at his heels. There was no time for talk then; all was instant action.

"As I was saying," the old one continued after they had both stopped, "the whip is a formidable entity." He paused to catch his breath. Then, "did you see how I took off before the crack came?"

The young one nodded.

"That was because the whip telegraphs. The lunge whip especially."

"The what?"

"The lunge whip, son. That is the long stick you have just witnessed in action. It lets you know it is coming before it makes its point. You can hear it. The lash lifting in the air makes a slight "whoosh" sound before the crack is heard or the sting is felt. This is what you learn from experience. It should then become knowledge. Now you know."

The colt nodded again. Something had changed. He no longer felt like running; not at that moment anyway. The words of his father were beginning to hold some interest for him. Even the zigging zagging yellow wings could not take him away.

"I see I have your attention," the grey continued. "There are two other sticks employed by the humanoid and each one says something about the user. It is not as they believe, that the whip is limited to one expression and that is: "get going, horse." For remember this, young fellow: the whip is the intent of the human mind. Whether it is a lunge whip, a dressage whip, or a crop, they will all tell you where the humanoid is coming from, if, and this is a big if, you know how to read them."

The young ones attention drifted for a second but came right back again. This must be what he had heard some of his buddies talking about. They called it a lesson. They said that all the old horses did it and that sometimes it could be worth standing still for. He wasn't sure about that, but for the moment…

"As I mentioned, there are two other sticks used by the humanoid: the training whip and the crop. And just why does the humanoid feel compelled to use such devices? Because he feels inadequate."

"In what?" This was getting confusing.

"Inadequate. It means that at base, most of them don't feel able to cope with being alive. I know that sounds like a foreign concept to you at this point in your life, but it is nonetheless reality."

"Dad, let's get back to the sticks. I think I'm with you there." He gazed up into the long branches of the willow in the low end of the pasture and had the passing thought that they resembled the sticks in question. He guessed there were sticks everywhere.

"And so these whips make the humanoid feel more comfortable, living as he does in a constant state of fear. They give him confidence when he has none of his own."

The colt allowed the words to enter him but he was still confused.

"But why do they feel that way? What's the big deal about being alive? It's easy. I do it every day" his youth was again asserting itself.

"Do you remember the bot fly and the electric fence?"

The young one shuddered at the words.

"This is our reality. The 'Zap' of the bot fly, the 'Zap' of the electric fence, and the 'Zap' of the whip of whatever type, all have an influence on us, at least for a brief time."

"It doesn't seem so brief though, Father. I still recall…"

"Yes, and that is the power of 'Zap.' It stays with you. You will always recall."

Here the two creatures paused to nibble at the newly sprung blades of grass. It was a beautiful spring day and they both were in need of a momentary diversion. Now that the whip-carrying girl had left, all was welcome calm. They sauntered about a small area of the pasture, always staying close. The red colt was beginning to watch his father. Not only his words, but the way he moved was interesting. He seemed to know absolutely everything.

After the two had eaten, they stood together. The young one relaxed and dropped his neck and head like his father. He also slowed the movement of his short, stubby tail. He was at rest and it felt good.

And so the two of them stood almost motionless in each other's company for several hours. The young one let go of his recent memory and the old one brought to the fore what he would next say to his son. Each had a responsibility: the young one to rest so he could learn; the old one to rest so he could teach.

When they returned from their welcome respite, they were renewed. The wise grey began.

"Though you have not felt the whip yet, trust me, it can be quite a 'Zap.' And it can be repeated as many times as the humanoid deems necessary. Given their proclivity for non-reason when fearful, it can become quite a barrage."

"Father, your words are sometimes so confusing. What is a bar-age?" The colt asked hesitantly.

"A barrage is an unremitting attack," the old one answered.

" A what?" came the plea.

"An attack that has no boundaries, no end, and makes no sense. In other words, the object of the barrage is unheeded. It is a one-way message from the attacker, an emotional unloading of the humanoid onto our bodies causing great pain, complete confusion, and distress for there is nothing we can do in return but flee. There is no choice."

"You mean, the whip can be used more than once? Like being 'Zapped' by a thousand bot flies, one right after the other, or becoming entangled in an electric fence where the 'Zaps' never stop?"

"Exactly, son. Unremitting."

"That sounds awful," another deep shudder ran through the young ones body.

"You are learning, son. You have just had the experiences of two 'Zaps' and from what I've told you about the third, you can imagine and predict. That is how knowledge is attained; how you make it yours."

The colt had to think about that for a moment. It was a first for him, after all.

"Are we finished with 'Zaps' yet, Father? I want to move a little," he added coyly, turning his head to the side and stretching his long legs in an expansive walk.

"No, not yet. There is one more 'Zap' you need to know about and it is the most powerful of all, more powerful, in fact, than all the other three put together."

"Oh, no. How will I ever survive? I barely got through this morning between the buzz and the zing. I don't think I'm ready or will ever be ready. It's just too much," the adolescent pleaded.

Ignoring his son's plaintive voice, the wise one continued.

"The fourth and final 'Zap' also comes from the humanoid but when he employs this 'Zap,' we shorten his name and we call "human." It seems more appropriate for we have heard him use this term in a positive sense when referring to another member of his species. By and large, however, the term "humanoid" is most correct for it denotes the aimless, senseless, arrogance this species most often displays toward others."

"So the humanoid is not like us, Father?"

"My, my, no. His motives are self-driven and so his assumptions about life fall short, very short. In short," and here the old one chuckled at his own play on words, "he thinks he's the only one here."

"But what about us? And the cows? And the chickens?" The youth hesitated, "and the bot flies?" Again a shudder, though this time it did not take over the particular moment in which it was uttered. It was merely a logical addition to the list.

"Exactly, young man. What about all of us? Each and every one of us from the most minute to the most gargantuan?"

"The most what?" came the pitiful voice again.

"The smallest to the largest," the old man offered. "From fleas to elephants. Aphids to rhinos. Bot flies to horses."

"I get it, the *all*." Here the young one paused to think about what he had just said. He was somewhat surprised at what had just come out of his mouth. He didn't think he really knew it but suddenly, there it was. Where was it hiding before? And why did it emerge now when he was trying so desperately to pay attention to his father?

"Precisely, son." The father's words were comforting. "The all."

The pair had begun to move again, just for sheer pleasure. They were as one and so it was time for the old grey to complete his lesson.

"There is one more 'Zap,' my young friend, though this one is far different from the other three. It also comes from the humanoid but when he uses it, we call him "human" and it is good."

"A good 'Zap?'"

"Yes, son, a good 'Zap.' But, it is rare. In fact, most members of our species have never felt it. They know of its existence from stories passed around but for most, it remains an unrealized possibility." Here the old gent paused to clear his throat and calmly noted how the unseen breeze became manifest only when it moved something. Like the grass. Like the leaves. Like the 'Zap' itself.

"But I have known this 'Zap' and it is good. It is powerful yet kind, fast yet comprehensible. It is an action yet a picture; it is idea and reality wed. There is no doubt. It is all-knowing."

"It sounds mysterious," offered the young one. "And what is a mystery anyway?" He was confused by his own quick growth.

"Many years ago, when I was in my late youth, I was taken to new surroundings for further education. I had already been "broken," as the humanoid is fond of saying, but of course, was still in one piece." Another chuckle came from the old one; he had learned to love word play.

"I was in full-blown strength and full of myself. There wasn't a humanoid I couldn't back off or throw off if he were lucky enough to even be able to get on me. I was a terror, if I say so myself. It was my way or no way. And, I was smart enough to do it."

The red colt was pensive. No one could see it but he was maturing by leaps and bounds, and there was nothing he could do about it. It just came.

"Well, as I was saying, I was moved and I didn't know it then, but my life would be changed forever. I was about to meet a master."

"A what?"

"A master, son. This is a type within the species humanoid, the one with the good 'Zap.' He is as rare as wings on a snake but he, or in this case, she, does exist, and I have experienced her."

By now the colt was beginning to yawn. Nothing exiting was going on and his father's words were fading into the distance. He was drifting off. What did he need to know all of this for anyway? Right now he felt good and wasn't that enough? Wasn't he supposed to be living in the now? No histories, no forecasts? He was a horse, after all, always in the present. Or was he?

"'Zap!'" Came the wake-up. And again. "'Zap!'" And once more. "'Zap!'"

"Are you with me now?" Was the admonishment.

The young man was wide-eyed and had jumped further and further and further from his father at each blast. Who was this creature anyway? It could not be his father for his father was kind and nurturing. This one before him was explosive and unrelenting. He was a frightening apparition from hell.

"I see you are," came the low, soothing voice. "You cannot possibly experience everything in life, you must amass knowledge. And knowledge is gained from the past and from the future. That is how you can successfully stay in the now. The humanoid would have it that we are always in the now and while it may appear to them as such, what they don't see is that our now is the product of past and future; not merely biding time in the lazy "whatever." Some of them strive to be in the now but they forget. Now is not nothing. Now is all."

"I get the "all," Dad. Sometimes it seems like I'm zinging." (The young one had returned.)

"You are, son. And that is a good way to put it. The "all" is zinging. There, and there, and there, but always the same. And that is where the master is, and that is where I met her."

"What were you doing there, Dad?"

"I'm always there and so are all members of our species - but so is she. And that was a shock. From the other three 'Zaps' you at least get a warning before they strike, but not from this one. You see and hear the bot fly; you feel him nestling into your hide. You see the wire strands of the electric fence and hear them buzz. The whip you can see being carried and hear it rise through the air before it makes contact with you. But from the fourth 'Zap,' you get no warning at all. You cannot see or hear it but its effect is the most powerful of all."

"And pray tell, Father, what is this fourth 'Zap?'"

"The fourth 'Zap' is the master's mind. It is the only thing that moves faster than we do; we cannot escape."

"But that's frightening, Father. For that's what we do to be able to go on with our lives: we escape!"

"Yes, that's true, but from the master we have no need of escape. We are always protected. You remember I told you that the fourth 'Zap' is a good 'Zap' and indeed it is for the mind of the master is with us and for us. There is no separation from what we would do anyway. I found this out instantly for when I tried to get rid of her with a mighty bolt, she simply turned my rebellion into what they call a "movement.""

"I'm confused, Father. What is a movement? Don't we move all the time?"

"Yes, of course we do. That is our expression. That is our way. But this movement is the kind we make not when we are in fear but when we are in love. It is a dance and when we move in this way we are joyful. The humanoid has no idea of this dance but the master knows and instantly invites us to partake for it is hers too. This was my master's message to me when I tried to get rid of her. I could not refuse the invitation for it was what I would want to do anyway."

"You mean, she knew?"

"Yes, in some strange yet natural way, she entered into me yet was all around me too. There was no separation. It was almost as if she knew what was going to be anyway but stayed right with me in the ceaseless moment. And she came from what was; like us. No stopping though; no dwelling. Only passing."

"Would I like her, Father? I mean, would I have to be something else? I mean, older, bigger, smarter?"

"Absolutely not. You will understand her immediately. And you will stop questioning for all is laid out – as it should be. As we are, so she is."

The old grey could see that his son needed some time to relive the most recent message. The red colt's eyes were large and repeatedly closed and opened slowly as if by briefly shutting down his vision, the young one could keep his father's generous words from escaping. And so they rested.

Once our young student had taken possession of all that was given him, he returned to his father's side. He had grown into spreading his time rather than always dashing through it.

He began slowly. "This fourth 'Zap' then; how will I know it? I mean, how is it so different?"

"As I said, it is a good 'Zap.' It has to be for it is the one we ourselves possess: an ebullient kick high into the air, a playful lunge to the side, a loud snort from distended nostrils – the impulse itself. It is the same with the master though less visible. You will know it because there is nothing but. It is all around and within, and always. It is our dance, our celebration. And it is hers too. There is no separation."

The youth understood. His father was a very wise man.

"So be comforted, young rascal." The wise one winked in secret understanding. "Know that she is there, somewhere, sometime. You will know her instantly and forever, in the where and in the when. It will not be otherwise."

And thus the two went back to nibbling on the blades of grass which seemed longer than earlier that day.

Perhaps they were.

Dom

The human is a funny creature. He loves the word "domicile" because it connotes a comfortable place to be in. A domicile is safe and unchanging. It is a nest for the family.

He also loves the word 'domestic" because again, it means to him that all is for his pleasure and security. He has taken "wild" out of creature and created a subordinate toy to accompany him in his quests.

But when it comes to the word "dominate," however, the human gets a little nervous. It could, after all, be turned on him. He could be the one enslaved, degraded, discarded. How could he ever feel safe with this idea circulating about the universe? Clearly, he must be the one who dominates. There is no other way. And so the misunderstanding lives on.

Within the society of the horse, however, there is no misunderstanding. It is as if he were the etymological model for the origin of the prefix "dom" and he has adhered to this for centuries. He lives the true meaning of "dom" and from him we can learn.

Originally, the term "dom" referred to the idea of a house: a physical structure in which all members of the family or society coexisted. It was an enclosure meant to ensure the welfare of all within. It also clearly defined all within as members of a group set apart from other individuals or groups.

While the feral horse does not live in a house per se, he does operate within an unseen boundary, not imposed from outside but arising from within each individual horse. This is a kind of cellular knowledge provided to each horse which tells him where to be and with whom.

From the original meaning of the word "dom" as house, the word now evolves into meaning "home." From the bare bones of location, "dom" now moves into the realm of qualifying the meaning of existence within that enclosure. It now becomes a home, which is beneficial for all within. It ensures safety and belonging, and a connection to all others. The domicile is a haven.

For the horse as a prey animal, this is of vital importance. His continuation depends on it. He must be part of a cohesive group made up of like-minded members, all having the same goal: survival. There is no room for dissention here. In order for the herd to survive, the horse must survive. And in order for the horse to survive, he must be part of a hierarchy within that herd, no questions asked.

The final meaning of "dom" has to do with hierarchy. From enclosure and haven, the word now means family as a living structure. This is a unit made up of individuals, each with his own particular view of what it means to be alive. Sounds a little like the human species, doesn't it? But there are vast differences.

Both humans and equines live in groups and largely for the same reason: safety. And though the human is considered a predator, he is often beset by a creeping paranoia when faced with a challenge he feels he can't "dominate." The result is that he will choose to belong to the family where the old adage "safety in numbers" comes into play. However, he is quick to disagree and to assert his individuality, no matter what the consequence. His assertion of self often leads to dishonesty, deception, and the title of "renegade." The drive to be an individual has taken precedence over the drive to survive. He must overcome another at all cost. This is his identity and for him, to *get* is the measure of his success.

The horse, on the other hand, does not perceive existence as centered on himself but rather on others within the group. His assertion of self goes only so far and does not cross the boundary of invasion to do harm. His sense of self does not require it. He belongs because belongs is to *be*, not to *get*. His reality is peaceful coexistence for all and within that outlook is his assured survival. Ah, the horse. What a model for living.

And so what does this suggest about the role of the human when interacting with the horse? We come to the word "dominate."

In contemporary usage, the verb "dominate" carries a derogatory connotation. To dominate another means to put him down, consider him less, stupider, poorer, weaker, in need of a ruler. We are definitely missing something here: the whole meaning of "dom."

But the horse knows this and peacefully carries on its historical nuances of meaning with seeming indifference to our narrow interpretation. He is the embodiment of "dom." His operation is a trade-off between subservience which he gives, and protection, which he receives. The one who dominates here is not after power or self-aggrandizement. He is simply the one who knows. He is the one possessing the balance between individual and other. And he does it for the good of all.

When the human is with the horse, he would do well to keep in mind who the horse is without him, then find out how to become a part of this exemplary government. For "dom" is not law, not merely one over the other in a fixed hierarchy. It is a code of ethics which the horse subscribes to. We would do well to learn this wisdom of compassion.

The Aid Formula

Is there anything concrete about "feel?" Is there anything we can lay down in solid terms and talk about?

Most would agree that the language we use with the horse dwells in that uncertain and often imprecise realm of sensation. It is not spoken or written; it is not heard or seen. Rather, it is taken in through neuro-pathways and its message is sensed. This is not to say that feel is an any less intelligent way of receiving language than any other for it is the same brain the messages arrive in and it is the same brain that understands the "meaning" of these messages. But, the prejudice remains. It is the human who relegates feel to a lesser means of perception; perhaps because he is so poor at using it fluently and meaningfully?

Fortunately for the human, all language, no matter in what form or of what consistency, possesses its own particular logic and the language of feel is no exception. Inasmuch as its primary purpose is to communicate with another and to exchange with precision, even feel moves with order and predictability, understandable to both horse and human. The human, however, has to give it a chance; the horse is already fluent.

Because language exists in time rather than space, its definition resides in changing qualities rather than static imprints. Like music, its meaning relies on movement and the process of making that movement. Unlike painting, it is never fixed in space. We still need a vocabulary to speak of it, however, though this vocabulary describes process rather than outcome.

The aids, as we term them, are never static and basically send one of two messages: stop, or go. If we picture a door in front of the horse, it is either open or closed, allowing or curtailing. Even that most sublime movement, the piaffe, exemplifies this concept. The horse is told to go forward, then quickly not to go forward. The only place he *can* go is up! The first message sent is always "go;" the second, "stop." Since the aids are circular, always influencing and modifying each other, the movement continues. It is energy we are dealing with here; the creation and the shaping.

The aids per se are easy to name – the legs, the seat, the hands, weight, overall position – but not so easy to define. Here again, we have a definition that "rests" in a continuous process, not a fixed, captured frame. Much like life itself, by the time you name it, it has changed into something else. But we can confirm the properties or ways in which they operate.

There are basically three qualities to any aid we ever deliver to the horse: timing, duration, and intensity. Considering one without the other two will never result in a complete message. The aids, after all, carry a language and we need all three qualities present in order for that language to evolve and to quickly adapt to what our "conversational" partner may offer in response.

"Timing is everything" and this is certainly not less true when speaking to the horse. Timing has to do with the onset of the message and when it is given can create an all or nothing situation. If it is given at a moment when the horse cannot comply, he will do one of two things. If he is finely tuned, he will hurry and disrupt his gait (movement) in an effort to respond. If he is not well-schooled, he will ignore the request and proceed on in his own little world. Either way, the human has been shown to be ineffective in his delivering precisely because the aid was given at the wrong time. It must be given when the leg is off the ground, when the head and neck are coming out of position, not once the leg is planted on the ground or the head and neck are out of position. These are the only times when the horse has a chance to change: if you direct a part of his body that is already in motion. If there is no movement, he cannot change!

The second aid quality is duration. This measures how long the aid is given. A word of caution here: don't overstay your welcome. Whereas timing measures the onset of an aid, duration has to do with its cessation. Basically, the aids ask, but then allow. They should never maintain! And it is the ceasing of an aid that gives the horse time and space in which to answer your request. Your aids should never be in the way as they will discourage rather than promote.

Between a shout and a whisper is normally where conversation takes place and there are innumerable gradations available within these two extremes. The third quality of the aids then, is intensity. This is the "too much/not enough" dilemma whereby we are ignored. Our response to the offering of the horse was either not received or was grossly inappropriate. In either case, it was the intensity of the statement that provoked the reaction.

Normally, the intensity of an aid is dictated by what the horse offers. Your aid should be a response "in kind" to what is given by the horse. For example, if the horse presents you with a quality you feel to be 3.2 ounces, your response should be no more that 3.3 ounces in return unless, of course, it's a "wake-up" call to him. If all is well, your reward to him is the soft caress of your touch which reassures and makes him want to stay there and be with you. The caress is the ideal voice to strive for. Anything more proves the conversation has not been refined. And of course, it is the release, (even of the caress!) that opens the path for the horse.

In addition to the qualities of the aids, there is one other aspect of the aids to consider before implementing the formula per se and that is the interchange between the aids. Simply put, the "go forward" message is never given when the "be round" message is given and the "be round" message is never given when the "go forward" message is given. If two aids are applied at the same time – Oh, Oh, we are going nowhere here – the horse will lock up. Simultaneous aids produce resistance in the horse: the back will stop, the head and neck will raise, and the gait will necessarily become shorter. It is only by separating the aids that the horse can both travel forward and be shaped.

Separation of the aids is achieved by dovetailing. As one aid is in the process of ceasing, another is in the process of beginning. It is not effective to give one, then give another. This isolates them and to the horse, one has nothing to do with the other when in point of fact, the aids constantly relate to and modify one another in a circular fashion. And so the aids cannot be given simultaneously, neither can they be given in isolation. They must overlap, but just how is this done? We come to the "Aid Formula."

Sometimes there is beauty in a formula. It can provide the foundation, the security on which to build, but also allows for instant change above that base. It can be perfect: neither rigid not arbitrary, static or mundane. It can be the launch-pad from which utter understanding is a certainty since it does nothing less than speak creation. And thus it is the way of communication with the horse since it uses what he knows already: how to be in the moment.

The formula itself is actually quite simple and is made up of the following four parts:

- deliver the aid
- wait for the response
- judge the response
- readminister the aid to change or to maintain the response

...and, that entire process takes about one fortieth of a second.

The initial delivery of an aid is always quick, always decisive. It is a point-blank statement given to the horse, a request, if you will, but not a plea. And, it is not prolonged since longer aids do not activate movement but actually serve to prevent it.

Humans are notoriously impatient creatures so the second step in the formula is difficult: simply wait. Remember, you are not giving a speech here. This is a two-way conversation and for it to be a conversation, the other party needs time to have his say. Don't anticipate and don't pre-judge. Your time is coming...and here it is. You have just felt your horse's response and it is now time for you to evaluate. Did he give enough? Did he give too much?

Was he early? Late? Evasive? Noncommittal? Spooked? Your judgment here is crucial to the fourth and final step in the formula: readminister the aid. Needless to say, steps three and four require some prior knowledge of the particular horse and what is an acceptable response from him and what is not.

After the judgment then, comes the reaction. This will be either a correction in order to change what is happening, or an affirmation more of the quality of a caress to let the horse know he is doing fine. Either way, the judgment always comes first, then the physical illustration of that conclusion. We must ask ourselves if our request was answered totally, in part, or not at all. Only then will we know how to respond.

The aid formula then, is an attempt to codify what actually takes place during language and most particularly, when that language is employed in a conversation. It does not tell you what to say, only in what order this conversation must take place. To disregard any of the steps would be to demean both horse and human to mindless, mechanical beings, aimlessly "going through the motions." The formula, however, puts the two together so that each has a voice and the chance to respond particularly to what is offered. Anything other than this is a dictate or a silence and, most importantly, there is no exchange.

And so the aid formula becomes an untiring foundation upon which our meaningful conversation may travel. It is a conduit which shapes but does not limit. It becomes the "way" to a most personal dialogue. Both horse and human may partake, it is understandable to both; no translation necessary.

The Mêlée

Forgive me for writing this, but in the horse/human world, confusion abounds.

"Why does my horse act like that?"

"Why doesn't he do what I want?"

"How come he doesn't listen to me?"

Sound familiar? We should just hear what the horse is saying. Something like:

"Why is she always hanging off my left side?"

"Why does she keep batting her heels into my rib cage?"

"And oh, my poor mouth. I can barely remember how to eat with it after she's through!"

So what are we both missing here? The answer is: understanding. Neither human nor horse is listening to the other and of course, the result is less than fruitful for either creature. A mutually understandable language has not yet been discovered and until this happens, all will be "foreign" language.

To say that it takes countless years to become fluent in any language would be an understatement. There is always more: new vocabulary, more precision, greater refinement, and of course, impeccable timing. Mastery comes through desire and diligence. Only after this has been achieved by the human, can he begin to play with the language. By now, it should be a part of him, his native tongue, if you will. He will have discovered the language that the horse speaks already. Only now can he begin to think and act in terms of the mêlée.

Mêlée is an old French word used to describe a situation in which there is no semblance of order and "anything goes," as they say. (Sounds like what the horse presents us with, yes?) Originally it had to do with hand-to-hand combat in which confusion reigned, but gradually evolved in meaning to become: a mixture, a mingling, and finally, a medley. What is so interesting about the life of this word is that even its history portrays exactly what we do in every training session with our horses: bring order out of chaos. As such, it deserves examination as to how it works from the trainer to the horse, the two potential "combatants" in our arena.

Primarily, the mêlée is thinking: instant thinking followed by quick action. It occurs in every situation between horse and trainer where the horse is asked, gives back, and the trainer decides: Was the request fulfilled? Was it misunderstood? Was it entirely ignored? Only then does he know how to proceed without hesitation. In essence, he is taking what the horse is giving and using it to his own advantage. He is constantly sculpting the horse's offerings, hopefully for the better.

In short, the mêlée is the establishment of the trainer's order while in the process of communicating with the horse. As might be expected, this process is not static or entirely predictable but varies as it must, depending on what the horse offers. And, here is the catch. It is precisely what the horse offers that is the trainer's opportunity to train. In other words, his response is directed to what the horse does at any given moment, not to some illusion of what the horse should be doing. This requires that the trainer have an absolute knowledge of where he is going with the horse and mastery over the mental and physical techniques to get there. He must be able to adapt what the horse offers, quickly and assuredly, in order to fulfill a particular goal.

For example:

Your horse has an adequate shoulder-in to the right. His right hind leg moves somewhat to the left and forward, his rib cage yields softly to the left, and his neck and head curve in an unbroken arc to the right. The problem comes when you ask that right hind to do more, as in the half pass or haunches-in left. (The right hind is, after all, the problem child of the four legs!) Suddenly you are presented with chaos. The right hind goes against your right leg and steps through it to the right. The rib cage straightens, the back stiffens. The head and neck rise defiantly into the air.

The "more" you had asked for was in the form of a haunches-in to the left (or a half pass or a working pirouette). They all require that the horse move his right hind leg at least in front of his left hind, (shallow), or better yet, over his left. They also require a bend to the left with the horse looking in the direction of his movement. His rebellion has arisen from the difficulty of the right hind being even further away from what is needed, its inherent crooked path, and its reluctance to bear weight. Now what do you do?

In the tradition of the mêlée, you will begin with what the horse knows already: the shoulder-in right. And you will use the one element of that movement that the horse offers willingly and the one that is needed for the half pass and the haunches-in to the left: the movement of the right hind to the left.

Mention should be made here of any preconceived ideas about use of the arena that the rider may harbor. Get rid of them! The mêlée is riding the horse, not the arena. It will require that you take whatever the horse gives you and turn it to the lesson at hand. In other words, no test riding. Straight and bend, yes, but anywhere you can get it. Now back to the horse.

You will begin with the shoulder-in right, down the long wall, through the corner, and down center line. (You will need the space this offers.) Once you are on center line, all is calm, and the horse shows no signs of anticipating any change, you will do just that: You will change your directive. In motion, ask the horse to gradually bring his head and neck to the left, all the while maintaining the stepping left of the right hind leg. This is the likely time when the horse will resist and he will do so by going against your right leg. He is in effect saying: "I will give you my head and neck or my haunches, but not both. And here is your opportunity. Instantly, ask for a leg-yield to regain influence over the right hind and begin again to reposition the neck. This time, however, since you are most likely at or close to the wall, you will think "renvers" and proceed again to ask for hind left, fore left, hind left, fore left. Move back to the quasi shoulder-in right if the horse resists, (as he most likely will), to change your tactic.

Remember that the goal here is control over the right hind so do a half turn, suggesting to the horse that he is "off the hook," and proceed in shoulder-in left. Simple.

Once calmness has returned, preferably out of a corner, ask for haunches-in left. When the neck and head resist by moving right, turn it to a counter shoulder-in and proceed for several strides, and back to haunches-in left. If the horse is still sticky and adamantly refuses, use the next corner and try for a few steps of the working pirouette. By arresting the forward movement, you are likely to receive two or three steps with correct flexion, if not extreme bend, and a right hind traveling to the left. Stop immediately and reward. You have achieved an approximation of your goal.

The mêlée, then, is an answer and the beauty of this answer is that it is appropriate to all occurrences which our friend, the horse, may present us with. It is at all times a harkening back to the goal of exactly what we want to change in the horse. No "side-stepping" here, pardon the pun. We confront directly and immediately to "attack" a particular issue and we do it with the movements just used in our example: Shoulder-in, half pass, leg yield, renvers, haunches-in, counter shoulder-in, and pirouette. It is not the horse who makes the perfect movements but the movements that make the perfect horse.

Though the term mêlée originally referred to combat, it has now evolved to mean medley and has an air of play about it. If one request does not work, another will – and – the requests keep coming. The difference in mêlée thinking is that whatever the horse gives is addressed so we are starting from where he is already and simply building through logical and comfortable procedure. Nothing comes out of the blue here. It is already all within the horse; we are just linking it to something new.

And so the mêlée is a way of thinking about the training process. It is not an adamant prescription to which all horses must succumb. It treats each and every horse in the particular moment in which he is, honors what he offers, but instantly adds a request to the offering. Our two "combatants" have begun to flow together because what they are doing is a part of both of them. And both the horse and the human have something to say. Let's listen with both ears, keeping the movement flowing, and share the bounty of the mix.

Paradoxical Dressage

Dressage is the embodiment of paradox. Within its practice there abide seemingly antagonistic qualities, but qualities which actually serve to provide the substance on which dressage is launched. On first consideration this would seem to be impossible but just because a statement or practice seems contradictory, unbelievable, or absurd does not mean it may not actually be true in point of fact. For paradox is actually completeness; an aggregate of two seemingly opposite qualities. And this aggregate in turn contains balance: the constantly shifting and replaying of opposites, each tempering the other into a lively partnership of exchange and re-creation.

For the perfect visual image of paradox, picture the eastern symbol of Yin and Yang. Within the circle are two equally distributed opposites, each entering the other but each returning to the circle also. There is no confrontation, no separation, only flow. And it is the circle which contains, directs, and makes use of this energy. Paradox is balance resulting from the complimentary proportion of opposites. This is not a static position to be caught and locked in place, for balance demands continual negotiation and adjustment. It is the tight-rope-walk of existence.

And what more graphic tightrope is there than dressage? This is the combining of two dissimilar creatures, the un-grounding of the human, the servitude of the wild creature, the master/slave dilemma, and the genetic dictates of predator/pray behavior. What an impossible lot of contradictions to put together and yet, we do, in some measure.

The Person

For the human, position on the horse can often be a nettlesome problem. We are told we must stay in one position but then again we are told to go with the horse's movement. The answer is we must accomplish both, not one or the other and, we must accomplish both simultaneously. Position itself is formal and unyielding. This is the outward appearance, the outline without deviation. At the same time, however, the inward substance of that outline is flexible and absorbing. So at one and the same time we are able to balance between foundation, (the outline), and substance, (absorption).

Another pair of seeming contradictions is that the aids of the rider must be strong yet soft. Knowing beforehand that the most powerful aid we possess is the mind, it suddenly becomes clear that it is indeed possible to embrace both for it is the physical body of the rider that whispers to the horse with light and caressing aids. This is, of course, the ideal but suffice it to say that the horse who appears to be performing on his own is the one directed primarily by the mind of the rider. The mind is always firm; the physical body always gentle.

And finally, the language we speak to the horse is both constant yet vanishing. Aids delivered in this way tell, (the constant), but allow, (the vanishing). Unlike human conversation, the communication we have with the horse applies not just to his thoughts, but to his movement as well. For this reason there has to be an "opening" each stride to let the movement proceed forward but a "closing" each stride also to create a shape. Delivered in this manner, the aids become fugitives; always there but always leaving. And this of course occurs in about a sixtieth of a second.

The Horse

The horse, (and what we expect of him), also embodies several seeming paradoxes. For him, however, a paradox is not to be judged, but embraced. He is the perfect Yin/Yang circle where opposites reside together as compliments, not adversaries, as with the human.

The first paradox within the horse is that he must be strong, yet supple. This is not unlike the dilemma faced by the rider when he learns position on the horse. For the horse, however, the two do not seem antithetical since he is by nature an integrated creature. Opposites are not isolated or pitted against one another but are encouraged to coexist so that they combine to create that much coveted state for the horse: balance. He has no problem understanding that his solidity must be elastic for that is what allows his movement and movement for him is everything.

Another paradox within the horse is that inertia makes him heavy and movement makes him light. It wouldn't seem like it to us but the addition of energy and the movement it demands is not actually the creation of strength, but the creation of ever-moving particles that bubble up within the shape, lightly, and forever. The epitome of these seeming opposites is the classical piaffe. What greater wonder and amazement can the rider experience than the coexistence of the power required to execute the movement and the softness necessary to allow it to come into being. The piaffe is the quintessential paradox combining power and lightness, reality and mystery, earth and sky. Each stride transcends.

And finally, the horse must be bent to be straight. Given that there are no straight lines in nature, this is not easily understood. But since we are going to ride the horse, we must make him straight for his own well-being. And just how do we make him straight? Through bending his body so that his rear leg footfalls land directly behind his fore footfalls and are not offset inwardly or outwardly. This of course requires a slight flexion of the head and neck toward the direction of movement, and a slight yielding of the rib cage around the rider's inside leg. It should be stressed here that the rider's outside leg and hand are of paramount importance since they both limit the yielding so that we do not create a new crookedness within the horse. He has plenty naturally on his own.

Unfortunately for us, the horse does not fathom paradox. To him, all is as it should be and so he operates in his own world between quick, startled reactions at needed times and pedantic movement most of the rest of the time. This is his world and he does what is needed for himself.

When we ride dressage, however, both the horse and the human must change. It is incumbent upon each of us to come into a new balance providing stability for this new mythical centaur-like creature. And it is paradox we are reconciling to create this new balance for is not the very idea of a human atop a horse the grandest paradox of all? We seem an unlikely combination.

The Language of Live

Language is both around us and within us. It flows without meaning or intent, however, until it is given voice through expression but it is there nonetheless, occupying apace and spending time. It is, in this state, a possibility, not yet a reality. Language becomes manifest only when it is taken up and used, relying for its full existence on purpose. It is, in other words, a "language of live."

To the horse, this language is as much a language of action as it is of thought since for him, the two are inseparable. What is done is thought of; what is thought of is done. This is quite unlike our human language which relies on word, symbol, and reflection for its meaning. Ours is abstract, referential. The horse's, however, is manifest: the language itself is what it means. And it is for this reason that the language of the horse is so profound: it is in the moment direct and complete, containing none of the ambiguity or deception of our human language.

Sounds simple, yes, but to perceive as the horse does and to become fluent in his language requires a reversal in attitude and thought from most humans and that change is: the horse has a viable and complete language of his own that expresses his perception of what it is to be alive. It is no less, no more than ours; it simply is, and as such, not available to negotiation. The respect due all language is the respect for what is in earnest, what is particular to each existence, and what expresses live. How fluent we become in this language depends on the constant search for precise meaning and the constant practice of unblocked awareness. The horse is going to teach us.

Time and Space

In order to even begin to understand the language of the horse, we must first see him as he sees himself, that is, as an integrated being. For him, there is no segregation of senses, (the mind included), and whatever passes into his awareness is experienced with his entire being. What he thinks he feels and what he feels he thinks. All flows throughout him without hesitation or censor.

And just how does this happen?

The answer is in the marriage between space and time that makes them not separate, independent measures but a cohesive form, a continuum of "space/time." The two become inseparable. Just observe the horse. Who he is exists continually and without interruption. The leaf of hay on the ground is not only seven walk strides away, (space), but it will take him five seconds, (time), to reach it and that is far more time than it will take for the other horse, who is moving faster (time) with longer strides (space) to reach it. And so another leaf is sought, one more easily available and one that requires a lesser expenditure of energy.

So what the human species can only guess at, the horse knows and demonstrates throughout his existence: that time calculates space and space predicts time. The two reside together in emptiness until there is an awareness within that emptiness. That perception fills and in a sense, validates what was empty and gives it form. That form is far from static, however, and is on the path of constant change because the occupant is live. Through time the empty is full and through space it becomes manifest.

Time

Time is arbitrary. We as humans fool ourselves into thinking we can measure it and thus harness it, but time escapes. It is particular to time that it continues without regard for our feeble attempts at capturing it and holding it in place. It defies us in passing, looking neither forward nor back, just incessantly proceeding. Our history is gone, our future not yet here. Just where are we on this continuum? In the now, of course, the constant now. And that is exactly where the horse resides, the question of location being as much a question of time as it is of space. For him, that leaf of hay just out of reach is a goal achieved quicker (more effort) or slower (less effort) but it is time that never pauses though its occupant may. Time here is the playground on which all creation exists even if it seemingly never moves. It is still passing whether we acknowledge it or not.

For the horse, stability is in the now. He does not evaluate according to what has happened or what will happen, but according to what is happening. It is his honest presence in the moment which makes him "directable," but which also often stymies humans in their dealing with him, the human predilection for knowing before doing being so much a part of our species. He does not plan; we do. He does not oppress the moment; we do. He is not fearful of the future; we are. And it all has to do with his perception of time. For the horse, the present is permanent.

Space

Space is not so arbitrary. For the human, a great deal of time is spent marking, carving, and delineating patterns, lines, and borders. It gives us the illusion of permanence, order, control. We can see it and it appears fixed.

For the horse also, space contains security through position and position denotes rank. But for the horse it is movement that catches his eye, movement through space. In his case, individual identity is gauged by where he is in comparison to others at any given time. This is who he is.

The horse is a master of space. His entire government is based on how he perceives it and how he fills it, and it is boundless. From stillness to movement, his position is stated, is read, and has meaning to the others around him. He projects both his personal and his group identity at one and the same time through space and, it is precisely this ability to project and to read accurately that ensures the stability and cohesion of the herd. Without this precision within the language, the herd would fall into chaos. There is no room for misinterpretation.

And so just how does this language work?

Time/Space

As a plains animal, the horse exists not by limit but by the constantly possible. As might be expected, his language reflects this.

Our language cannot begin to express what his does, dependent as it is on past and future for its meaning. This is the time it takes for connection, and then for prediction, and then for reminiscence. Engaged as we are in this restless communication, we entirely miss the nuance of the present and skip from history to future, dragging one and dreading the other as if again, we could possibly master either. In the meantime, we miss the point: the now. We do not see, we do not hear. We merely fluctuate between unattainable positions, jumping back and forth over the expansive present.

On the plains, however, time and space are inseparable and this is the domain of the language of "live." This is where the horse lives and where his language operates: in the ever present. Both music and dance also rely on the ever-passing present for their meaning. Music moves through time, dance through space. Each define passage, not finiteness and it is precisely this quality that makes them somewhat elusive. To know them is to be always in the presence of the present. Unlike painting or sculpture where the message is static and unchanging, the inherent meaning in music and dance is change and hence, connection. From one note to another, one movement to another, there is no emptiness; all is filled. And likewise in dressage, the essence is change through time/space; in a word, flow. And the primary characteristic of flow is this: everything that moves makes a sound, and every sound moves. In this circular sense, movement is sound and sound is movement. The two are facets, not entities in and of themselves. Both exist through time and space at once, thus creating flow and it is flow that harkens back to the core of the horse and where he lives: in the open. To the horse, all is endless possibility without restriction.

Music/Dance

That same endless possibility is the hallmark of the time arts, music and dance. Both rely for their existence on change and while a work itself may be prescribed and preordained, no two performances are ever the same and so we are back to the language of "live:" that ongoing affirmation of existence.

It is no coincidence that many of the terms used in dressage are borrowed from the world of the time arts for it is in these arts that we attempt to express what it means to be alive. Terms such as harmony, balance, and rhythm all live through the time arts and as such, are particularly relevant to dressage. They define how the art means, not necessarily what it means since the meaning here relies on passage through time and change of space, and so it is with dressage. It is not the fact that the horse executes the piaffe but how he executes it. Is he rhythmic, balanced? Does he rise up from harmony within himself and with his rider? Do the two speak the language of "live?"

In dressage, what you see occurs simultaneously with that you hear. The eye perceives the picture, the ear the song. The eye evaluates space, the ear, time. The eye notes roundness or angularity, the ear, cadence or unevenness. Both come into play when creating the horse to form a complete entity, outside to inside. It is by virtue of the eye that we determine: in what direction? In what manner? In what shape? It is through the ear that we determine: in what rhythm? At what tempo? At what gait? But just how do we dance this dance? Sing this song?

The Aids

The aids are not cures. They are not mere stimuli that are associated with pain or pleasure which the horse learns after repeated exposure. Rather, the aids are the components of a delicate language which the horse already knows. The aids are the nuances of whisper and air, barely discernible – except to the horse. As such, the language of the horse is not referential but honest and direct. It is personal and it is present.

In order for the trainer to speak such a language, he must first believe that such a language is possible. Most of the time this requires a radical shift in the human view that we are the only ones on the planet with language. This is far from true. Ours may be more obvious but ours is a language of bombast with listening hardly possible. For the horse, this is anathema. The trainer must know this in some way and wish to connect with it. In other words, his must be a constant search for the lightest yet most potent way of address while all the time maintaining a fluent balance between demand and acquiescence. He must find the "soft spot" within each horse, the place of perfect balance between calmness and excitement where the horse is both receptive and responsive. This is the place of language; all else is noise.

The aids should make up a palpable language. As such, they are the enactment of the mind, the felt thought, the inside brought to opening. In this display, the idea becomes visible, audible, sensory. There is no separation between the mental and the physical: they have become the same.

For the horse, this is quite natural. What he is thinking, he is doing; what he is doing he is thinking. Note the present tense here for this is part of what makes this language unique: it is always immediate. It is not that the horse is faster than we are. It is simply that he is always in the present which many times comes as a surprise to us as we vacillate back and forth between what was and what will be. But for this language to work, we must change and change radically. We must become as quick as the horse, but no quicker.

Common knowledge has it that the aids move only one way: from rider to horse, done. This is quite erroneous and smacks of the master/slave relationship where an order is given, an order is obeyed. But linear thinking robs the aids of their potential for reciprocity which is at the heart of the way in which language works. Language is a continuum passing from one to the other, always moving. Though the sender and the receiver change identities frequently, the language continues, upheld by both without lag. Sounds good in theory but just how does it work in practice?

Each component of a live language consists of the following structure:
- Stimulus
- Response
- Analysis
- Stimulus if needed
- Response

It matters not whether the human or the horse is speaking: the structure is the same.

If the horse were initiating the conversation, it would go something like this:

Horse nudges standing human for a treat.
Human backs up, surprised.
Horse thinks, "That didn't work. I'll try again."
Horse nudges harder the second time.
Human extends carrot to the horse.

Of course, the horse doesn't always come out on top but by nature he will try to find his position in the relationship and try again. His language is quite clear to the human even though no words are used. His language is the perfect melding of thought and action, the language of live.

The human must also follow this "natural" structure, the only difference being, he has to learn it first. The horse is waiting to be understood and to understand.

And so the fluent human would begin the conversation like this:

Human asks horse to stand quietly and wait.
Horse moves shoulders out of line with his haunches.
Human thinks, "That is not what I asked: I'll realign him."
Human moves horse's shoulders back into position.
Horse realigns shoulders but quickly moves out of position again.

Obviously, in this case the language was understood initially but not obeyed totally. Note though that whether or not the request was fulfilled totally or partially, it was in both cases understood. And this is the beauty of this language: it needs no translation so it cannot be misinterpreted. In this sense, it becomes a statement of existence, direct and non-referential and, it is always being practiced and refined. Persistent and ongoing. Does this not sound like life itself?

Conclusion

As understood by the horse, the language of live expresses thought and action and in turn becomes the manifestation of existence. This is where the horse lives and where he comprehends his being and his world. This is his vision, his reality. In a sense, it is reminiscent of a metamorphosis from the physical to the non-physical, a transformation, if you will, where language becomes existence, not just a metaphor for it.

And so in this synthesis there is no separation between thought and action but a melding of the two that marks intent. This language is not apart or other than, but present, viable. It is, in essence, the "language of live."

The Three Ts

Here's the Human

When we choose to partake of the study that is classical dressage, we are offered a unique possibility on our journey through life: no other endeavor places us in such closeness to a fellow creature. We think, we feel, we join. We even surrender physical security on our own two feet and leave it up to the horse! And of course, the horse is always right. This is one of the great gifts he can give us and one we would do well to accept graciously. And through this realization, growth is assured; it is not a choice.

Within the experience there is always more: a new height, a new depth, and ultimately, a passing and an entering – and so it is. This journey can travel in many directions, assume many shapes, and rest at times on a particular level, but the essence is far greater. That essence is change, and change is the way. There is no other.

Here's the Horse

"Son, do you believe in change?"

"What is there to believe in? It is. I mean, it's not a question of belief. Sometimes, father, you sound so human. I don't get it."

Here, Helmut chuckled and moved his tail slowly, calmly, from side to side. He was quite old by now and had seen much in his life but more importantly, had thought much. What else was grazing time for? Something else had to happen besides mere munching.

"Forgive me, son, but there is one more lesson for you to learn and it occurs to me that today would be a good day. I'm in an expansive mood and it is early enough; all is peaceful." Here Helmut stretched his dappled body down into a long bridge and slowly brought it together again, refreshed. Old age had its requirements.

"Father, honestly, I'm not in the mood. I'm off to try and catch a glimpse of Penelope in the next pasture. She's oh, so stunning, and she seems to like me."

Our young man, Dodge, had become a teenager. Though he had been well-educated by his masterful father, (and he excelled at his studies!), he was still a teen and there were uninvited awakenings occurring within his body. It wasn't his fault. It was just the way things were. Change, you know.

"Dodge, you will have plenty of time for that. Right now it is your education I am concerned with and there is one more lesson I wish to give you. It is the lesson of "The Three Ts.""

"You mean like what Penelope does to me? Tease?"

The senior laughed. "No, son."

"Then you must mean what humanoids sip from cups? Teas?"

"Not quite, This "T" is the letter "T" and it begins three words that together form the subject of your next lesson."

"Oh pray, father, what will that be?"

Dodge could not help but interject a bit of sarcasm into his question. Even though the years had made him a serious student, he was still a teenager and given the chance, "bucked" authority.

Helmut rolled his eyes but said nothing at first. He knew what he was about to reveal to Dodge was not commonly discussed but he also knew that his son was ready if not eager. He would wait. Stretching his long, lightly dappled neck to the ground, he began to selectively pick at choice blades of pasture grass. Some were indeed better than others; it was all about knowing.

Dodge followed his father's example and began to graze. He had always wondered why some mouthfuls were tastier but he, on the other hand, supposed it was just chance. Lots of life was like that; just a matter of chance.

"This subject is different," Helmut began, "for it describes a kind of evolution."

"Evo – what?" The young man's mouth was full.

"You remember. Eohippus, mesohippus, modern horse."

"Oh, ya. Change again."

"Precisely son. And so we come to the lesson of "The Three Ts.""

Dodge remembered the story of his ancestors and how they were little, little, little. How lucky they were – closer to the grass! He munched peacefully and waited for his father.

"The three Ts begin words that describe the three stages of a particular evolution. In this case, mine."

Dodge quickly flipped his ears toward his father and stopped chewing.

"Once, I was a human."

Dodge dropped his lower jaw and his beloved grass fell in a wad to the ground. He was stunned. Who was this creature standing before him? What was he saying? Why did he have to say it right now when the lovely, green blades were oh, so delectable? Dodge was angry now.

"You've lost it, dad, or whoever you are. What on earth are you saying? You're hallucinating. Or you've found some of that special weed like in the next field. How can you even think something like that? I just don't know you anymore."

By now Dodge was in a kind of lather but the outburst couldn't stop him from feeling betrayed. A tiny bead of water crept down his face. He had never felt that before and briefly wondered where it had come from.

Helmut waited, then slowly walked over to his son and stretched his neck over his son's neck. The stood quietly like this for some time, in each other's care. They were folded, never-ending.

And again, the wise one waited and watched. He knew the time was always right. But he also knew there were opportunities to slip in and hardly be noticed. Now was that time.

"Yes, Dodge, once I was a human," he began again.

The young one slowly raised his head and neck and gazed at his father through moist eyes.

"Why are you telling me this?" Dodge began quietly. And then, slightly stronger, "why do you always think I have to know something?" And again, more pitifully, "it's been this way my whole life."

Helmut was quiet for some time, respectful. He then offered, "because you need to know."

It was always this way. Always more. Always something else. Always something other than. Always, always, always. Why didn't anything ever stay the same? Just like the butterflies. They never stayed put. At least you could count on grass. It was always the same.

Helmut continued. "As a human, I had always loved horses and been drawn to them. I did not understand it then but I followed my heart, as humans are fond of saying, and took any opportunity to be close to them, or us, as the case may be." Helmut chuckled softly. "Are you with me, son?"

"I th-th-th-think so." (The three Ts!)

"As a human I took many detours along the way but finally found myself in a position to learn about what I so passionately loved: horses. By then I was thirty."

"That's so old, father."

"Not for a human, son. They, or I, in this case, mature slowly if at all. The paths are many and deceptive. As a human I went forward, went back, went to one side, went to the other, went to the future, went to the past, started over – you get the picture. The journey was not simple then but as I look back, it should have been. I was really after only one thing even though I couldn't even name it then. Not that I can now either. I had never even dreamed…"

Dodge listened but with only one ear cocked. His initial astonishment was beginning to wane and he wanted activity, not some stay-still-and-listen diatribe. Oh, where was it all going anyway? This growing up thing was definitely tedious.

"So at thirty I met a Master," the old one continued, "and a Special Horse."

Dodge looked at his father with questions already forming. "Aren't all horses 'Special?'" was the first.

"Yes, of course all horses are "Special" but remember, I was a human then. Juxtaposition of circumstance was all-important."

There he went again. Using big words.

"What I mean is, the Master and the Special Horse came into my life at the same time. I was allowed to partake, and I was ready."

"Ready for what?" Dodge interjected. He wasn't hooked yet and thought a little snide comment would be appropriate.

Helmut waited for the moment to pass, then began again.

"All my life I had been drawn to horses but was never quite satisfied with what I knew about them or how I lived with them. And then it happened. The first "T:" Transmit. I was literally being sent information by both the Master and the Special Horse. It was up to me to take it in and this I did over years."

Dodge tuned in again. Momentarily, his belly was not "sending messages" to him.

"The Master was a stern sort and well-versed in the conventional beliefs of the day. This is not to say that he didn't know what he was demonstrating. He did – at least in light of the history of humans and compared to others of his ilk. He was indeed a Master according to human definition. I took in all that I could from him, faithfully practiced what he gave me, and became quite adept at accomplishing the goals before me. I was beginning to "produce" the horse, as the human is fond of saying.

"And how can you produce something that's already there?" came the query. Dodge was actually beginning to listen to his father's language. He was almost a full-fledged adult, after all.

"Exactly, son. And that is what I learned. The horse already knew how to be a horse. I, the human, was the one who was woefully ignorant. And this I learned not from the Master, but from the Special Horse. The Master, after all, was on the plane of opposites. You know: big and small, us and them, good and bad. And he took the horse with him, ignoring what was there already. Instead, he placed us within this human construct of arbitrary standards and justified accordingly."

"You mean, he ignored us?"

"Yes, in a sense. He thought what he was doing was right though. And, to give him credit, he was the best of his kind."

"Then how did you escape this outlook? I mean, you were only human." Both horses laughed.

"Exactly. And I would have stayed within that limitation if it were not for…"

"The Special Horse?" Dodge was on the journey now.

"Yes. The Special Horse. And he was the one who brought me to the second 'T:' Transform."

Both horses were silent. Dodge was heavy with thought. Oh, just where was this going? Weren't all horses "Special?"

As if Helmut heard the thoughts of the young progeny, he began again. They were on the journey, after all, and to stop would be illusion.

"And so I practiced and drilled, over and over and over. This went on for a substantial amount of time as if the sheer time spent was the most important ingredient to becoming a Master. The idea was that there was something to get, something to achieve. I was about to become aware of a totally different reality. In other words, the better I got, the less convinced I was that this was the way."

"And how come you felt like that, father?"

"The change happened one bright, sunny day when I was out in a large, grassy field, schooling the 'Special Horse.' I was repeating over and over again what I had learned but I was dissatisfied. I couldn't get the reaction I wanted. Something was missing and no amount of diligence seemed to be helping. I was at an impasse, to say nothing of my 'Special Horse.' We were on different planes, if you will. I wasn't getting to him and he was ignoring me."

"So what did you do?" Dodge offered. "You know I'm still getting used to the idea of you talking as a human. I have to keep reminding myself. I mean, what could you do?"

"You're right on the mark, Dodge. I did nothing."

They were silent again. Dodge sent his eyes toward any precious new blades within his reach but didn't follow through. Helmut deliberately let his eyes go fuzzy in remembrance for a moment, then returned to the immediate.

"And then it happened." Helmut paused, not certain how to continue. Summoning his courage, he went on.

"I began to listen and to feel. The Special Horse had entered me. I left off drilling and experimented. I halted mindless repetition and began to create. I did things out of order, out of sequence, out of standard, but I was always directed by the Special Horse. And I in turn directed. He was giving me the language and I accepted joyfully.

And so we passed into one another. And through and through we went, always flowing, ever one. It was as if I was talking to myself in another form."

This was a lot for Dodge to absorb but he did know about herd life where all members moved as one. How it happened he had no clue. He just knew it was. It was not a mystery; it was the way.

And then it happened.

"And then it happened," came Helmut's voice. "The third 'T:' transcend."

Oh, this must be the end of the story, thought Dodge. All of this fluttering back and forth had to have an end, didn't it? It was time to return to the beckoning blades, after all. They were just waiting. Or were they?

"So through my two-legged years I went, pedestrian on the ground, almost avian when on my Special Horse. One day when we were particularly together and all was clear and all was certain, all was ahead but only slightly, and only then and then, and on and on – from here (or there), there was no turning back. I began to soar and to gallop and to frisk and it was all quite natural. I was in rhythm, in tempo with, and part of. And so here I am before you."

Dodge looked but could see no difference. It had always been this way. He was waiting for the surprise, the "Bam," the "Wow" – like Penelope in the next pasture. Now there was something to be bowled over by.

And so the two strolled down to the far end of the pasture where they could pick peacefully and "digest." The sun was losing its intensity to be slowly replaced by the moon and all was well with the exchange.

"Oh, and one more thing, son. If I could still speak my former language I would say: I am transcended. I am horse."

And indeed, here he was.

About the Author

"Go forward, be round" is a philosophy frequently heard at Hermitage Dressage, Winchester, Wisconsin. Expressing the essence of the classical ideals of riding, this phrase has become the signature of Susan Medenica's training and instruction.

Susan Medenica has worked with a wide variety of students and horses over the years, always striving to expand the unique talents of each. Whether starting the novice horse or rider or polishing the more advanced, the integration of one with the other is always the guiding principle.

A lifelong student and practitioner of the Classical Arts of music, literature, and riding, Ms. Medenica has also created two special educational opportunities for the serious rider: the "Open Training Sessions" and "Readings on Dressage." The first is in clinic format with all lessons geared toward a central theme. The second is essentially a book club which explores the past and present body of literature on classical riding.

www.ingramcontent.com/pod-product-compliance
Lightning Source LLC
Chambersburg PA
CBHW020110020526
44112CB00033B/1123